The Listening Walk

The Listening Walk

40 poets

Editor: Sue Boyle
Copy editors: Stephanie Boxall, Linda Saunders
Section editors: Ama Bolton, Stephanie Boxall, Sue Boyle,
Rosalie Challis, Claire Dyer, Deborah Harvey,
Rosie Jackson, Linda Saunders
Cover painting: Malcolm Ashman

Bath Poetry Cafe

First published by Bath Poetry Cafe in 2013.
sueboylepoetry.wordpress.com

COVER PAINTING
Malcolm Ashman RBA ROI
Chalk Down, Dorset
oil on board, 2011

ISBN: 978-1482558678

A CIP catalogue record for this book is available from the British Library.

A year of good poetry

The Bath Poetry Cafe is one of those essential organisations that spring directly from a love of poetry and work brilliantly to enable others to write, read and above all hear poetry. Long may it flourish!

Michael Mackmin

The Rialto

The Bath Poetry Cafe is one of those ventures which grace the city. Showcasing the best of poets, workshop leaders and editors, it encourages the writing and reading of poetry. Events are open to all poets, from the beginner to the more experienced scribbler. That they are successful can be seen from the poems in this volume. Would that every town had its own Poetry Cafe.

Patricia Oxley

Acumen

Bath Poetry Cafe poets are a creative and driven group who write, promote and encourage the best poetry. They make poetry an event.

Allison McVety

Miming Happiness, The Night Trotsky Came to Stay

Bath's Poetry Cafe events are so varied and stimulating that it's splendid to discover that something of their refreshing flavour has been preserved in an anthology like this. *The Listening Walk* is a delightful distillation from a year of these poetic and professionally creative activities; it offers an irresistible invitation to all who haven't yet discovered what poetic pleasures are to be found in this lovely city.

R V Bailey

Course Work, Marking Time, From Me to You
The Losing Game, Credentials

Contents

Foreword

The 40 poets whose work appears in this anthology were all part of a remarkable series of events celebrating poetry in 2012, the year of the Cultural Olympiad. Poets from Bristol, Reading, Swindon, Malmesbury, Taunton, Wells, Glastonbury, Weston-super-Mare, Chippenham, Frome and Radstock, as well as from Bath and surrounding villages, shared regular Writing Days in the Bath Royal Literary and Scientific Institution (BRLSI) in Queen Square. In April, many of them also attended a day of talks, readings and discussion with Bloodaxe editor Neil Astley. In June, Patricia Oxley, editor of the Torbay literary journal *Acumen*, chose the winners from our competition shortlist during an evening of good food and guest readings in the BRLSI's glamorous Elwin Room.

One of the most remarkable events of the year was the collaboration between Cafe members and three well-known portrait artists – Malcolm Ashman, R Scott Fraser and Ben Hughes – who are engaged in a three-year project to record the faces of Bath. Cafe poets visited the artists in their studios, sat for their portraits, wrote about their experiences and contributed some of the resulting poems to a multimedia evening show in November. The readings, combined with slide projection and recorded sound, drew an audience of more than 80 people. Some of the poems have made their way into this anthology. Cafe poets also contributed group performances to the days of poetry at the Bath Literature Festival and the Wells Festival of Literature.

This year of events was generously supported by Bath & North East Somerset Council and by Poetry Can in Bristol, and we are all very grateful to B&NES Arts Development Officer Peter Salt and Poetry Can Director Colin Brown, not just for their financial assistance, but for their continuing encouragement and support for the Bath Poetry Cafe.

Sue Boyle

IF A POET LEAVES HER BODY TO SCIENCE

suppose what is found within is poetry –

lodged in every dissection, scored into cell walls.
Along the fissures of the cranium, scribbles

grafted onto bone; words embedded in the walls
of arteries, tucked taut in organ membranes

as if secreted into pockets. Prepare to be moved
by a love sonnet holed up in the vast atria of the heart

or a bright refrain floating in the dark rafters
of the ribcage like a song thrush in high branches.

And suppose in the lobes of the brain, synapses
are threaded together by filaments of delicate verse

or in the bowel, a churn of dog days doggerel.
In the spiral corti organs, listen out for villanelles!

Anticipate pert haiku inked in spinal fluid
onto vertebrae and wistful cantos hiding in the eyes.

There'll be surprises, like a rondelle round the belly.
Mighty waterfalls of free verse, erstwhile gushing,

may be pooling in the kidneys. Look!
Her soles – the imprint of the tread, the tread,

the rhythm of persistent feet. Release the rap
from silent lips. And what's that final resonance

that catches on the tongue's cold tip? Ghazal?
Once you have noted all – don't analyse, don't stress.

Write your post mortem: here's a poet,
(mock heroic), who composed herself;

whose life's worth is the paper it is written on –
a body of work. No more, no less.

Janice Booth

1

In a Year's Turning
Deborah Harvey

Throughout the drive from coast to moor I'd been peering out of the car window, trying to gauge which way the weather might turn and clinging to every shred of sailor-blue sky between cloud. Now, as we parked on the sparse turf edging the strip of tarmac that passed for a road, our first waymark, Frenchbeer Rock, loomed like a cross-Channel ferry plunging through murk.

'You were the one who wanted to come,' grumbled Spouse as I dithered. 'It's up to you whether we walk or not.' We set out across choppy grass. With each step the sky grew darker. At Middle Tor I heard the first plops of rain on my hood, and by the time we'd reached the bulk of Kestor Rock, a wall of water was rolling towards us from the west over open moor. We pressed ourselves against its granite ramparts. Four sets of beleaguered eyes gazed up at me through jagged, dripping fringes. A dewdrop dangled from Spouse's nose. There was nothing to lose. I stripped off my now sopping cagoule, spread my arms like aeroplane wings and started to chug around the outlying boulders. 'Come on, kids!' I yelled. 'There's no point trying to shelter any more. We might as well have some fun!'

While liberating, it is not always practical to surrender so completely to the elements, something I pondered at length on the teeth-chatteringly cold journey back to our caravan by the sea. That said, it is vital for our physical and spiritual well-being to get outside whenever we can to observe what, in Poem in October, Dylan Thomas terms 'a year's turning' – namely, those shifts that herald the varying seasons, some marked, others more subtle, but all muffled by our double-glazed, thermostatically regulated way of life.

Here poetry can help, especially on those occasions when we are bound, by obligation or fatigue, to the routine turning of that other great wheel, the treadmill of daily living. It might be freezing February out there beyond our UPVC windows, but by evoking colour, sound, odour and taste, a poem can transport us to a Spanish garden or tide-tickled shore in summer, dusky bluebells in not yet long grass, or a wilderness of weeds. It can summon kingfishers, starlings and pheasants; feed us wild strawberries, chanterelles, pearls and blood; light a bonfire underneath our torpor.

When we write about nature, we are reminded that we are all part of a whole in which no one element is more important than any other. With their delicate, precise and often startling imagery, these seasonal poems reinforce this understanding, at the same time enabling us to see – as if for the first time – catkins patterned like snakeskin, tantalising foetal clouds, the fractal branches of trees. We especially know that we are experiencing the world with all of our senses engaged when even the mundane becomes extraordinary, as in this arresting image from Rachael Clyne's Grounded:

> *twin-bead headlights travelling to and fro.*
> *Red corpuscles for Glastonbury, white for Wells.*

Nor are our own human seasons neglected. In Room, the poet looks back to a childhood filled with scent, sound and warmth, and, like Remembrance, recalls a dead father. It is the turn of 'soft-cheeked' youth to explore love in Spring, and both Patrick Walking and Beatitude examine the challenges that come later in life, the former describing the process of healing, the latter a moment of clarity in the now clouded mind of a mother. Finally, in her accomplished villanelle, Twenty Seven, Elinor Brooks considers the way even memories wear and change with the passing of years.

So, as the opening poem, Lichen, exhorts us, let's abandon human maps and follow the markings on stone and bark. We can don our hideous pink hats, travel by punt or take the first foot-ferry of the year, carve a path through pollen and stubble, then wait, marvelling, for the animals to come. It's only a matter of time.

LICHEN

I am done with human maps,
their endless contours
of concrete and invasion.

Give me these markings on stone and bark,
their flowers, marriages,
mosaics of weathering.

Teach me their codes of survival:
the wild alchemy that knows how to transform
air and moisture into beauty

that drapes this coloured quilt –
thrift pink, egg blue, citrus green – over granite,
weaves this patterned complexion into wood.

Let me study lichen,
the pioneer that knows how to build
spaces others can inhabit

that needs only to be left alone
in pure wind, through unhurried time
to know the way forwards.

Rosie Jackson

INEVITABILITY

The quiet tide tickles the shore.
A mermaid afternoon, mild and mellow.
The mountain shadows, summer must end.

The tide turns dark.
Its depths dream of winter.
Hear the ice song clear and stark.

The west wind welcomes the child year
with spring on its breath.
Grass again in the valley.

Magnet-drawn the river enters the sea.

Beryl Kellow

IN A SPANISH GARDEN

for Lindsay Blyth

Shaded by a pomegranate tree,
the Guyanan hanging-seat
is an oasis
of coolness
in this intense
blue heat.

Borders as luminous
as Matisse's palette
entice the sybaritic breeze
with the perfumes
of a paradise regained
from brambles and neglect.

Beyond the swimming pool,
terraces fall to an English lawn,
avocado and lemon,
orange and mandarin,
plum and fig,
and numerous nut-bearing trees.

In a dried-up gulley gritters
gnaw fallen hazelnuts
as foetal clouds
above the serrated horizon
tantalise
the parched red earth.

This morning irrigation water
escaped
from a neighbour's confining walls,
teasing the garden
with an illusion
of rain.

Jeremy Young

WEEDING LESSON

Faced with a wilderness of weeds,
first find a way in.

Carve a path, like a river, with tributaries
branching in different directions.

Choose two or three of the biggest,
most vigorous, variety.

Trace them back to the base,
place the fork just in front. Plunge in.

Rock back and forth to loosen the weed –
on more than one side if necessary.

Then, reaching down, feel around
for the root, and tug.

If it doesn't come, go deeper, following
the root with your fingers till you have a purchase.

Ease it out of the ground, taking care
not to damage the surrounding plants.

You won't get them all but, gradually,
you will assert your supremacy.

Or so you will believe.

Stephanie Boxall

RADICALS

The trees spin traceries
of sugar in their leaves

send symbiotic sweetness
through the forest floor
to fungi barely within reach

whose secret juices
break down particles of soil
prepare a feast

hyphae spread their mantle
fungal threads ensheath
the roots of trees

and leaf mould covers the embrace
of tree and fungus joining at the tip
to lace the cup of each

across the kingdoms –
Scots pine to chanterelle
chanterelle to fern-leafed beech –

the trees are spinning
sugar under ground.

Elinor Brooks

Man should... whisper... to his neighbour
and thus... every human might become great,
and Humanity... would become a grand
democracy of Forest Trees.
Keats to Reynolds, February 1818

REMEMBRANCE

skeins of starlings stream towards the reeds
swooping and settling as the marsh harrier soars above
them
late-comers fly in to join the multitude
their chattering like music, a hidden hymn
rising briefly in a dark cloud, they emerge and settle
a blackbird calls and all are still and silent
as dusk falls on Armistice Day

Venus shines bright and low over Glastonbury Tor
north star twinkles high overhead
and we walk home listening
to the reeds whispering
seeing the red lights of the aerial mast
talking of our dead fathers, their shared history
in the signals during the war
wearing our red poppies
wishing for peace

Morag Kiziewicz

FIRE

Wreathed in fog he stands by the fire.
Smoke hangs heavy in the damp air,
but he knows fire,
knows how to kindle
the carefully guarded tinder and twigs;
how to draw it up,
how to feed it,
yet keep it hungry.
Knows how to smother it a little,
make the flames hunt for fuel.
He layers sticks and stalks,
thistles, teasels,
forks on a mattress
of privet and buddleia clippings.
He knows how to keep the heart hot.
Seed-heads escape, blaze, spiral,
fire flies in the night.
The fog retreats a little and
I join him with wine.
Coats steaming we raise a glass
to last year's growth; watch,
as it blossoms for the last time.
Kiss.
Tomorrow he will spread the cold ash
around the brassicas.

Linda Perry

GROUNDED

No red buttons on the Mendip Mast tonight
it being damp and cloaked in softest grey.
Thick air hides the ridge, blurring sky and ground.

Just the satellite wink of headlight traces
what seems to be sky: a road high in the hills.
Snow is forecast so I expect to wake

to icing sugar sprinkling the slopes.
Meanwhile the vague monochrome
of the combe lies ghostly below.

Beyond, a delicate web of sodium
marks the edge of town
yellow cobweb floating on moist grass.

A thin vein threads Glastonbury to Wells
across the blanked out Levels, lit only
by twin-bead headlights travelling to and fro.

Red corpuscles for Glastonbury, white for Wells –
its twinkle cluster in the distance.
Tonight, all the stars are on the ground.

Rachael Clyne

OPEN WINDOW

So much depends upon
colour
light
scent

Stalagmite grass blades stand to attention
water course halted by winter breath
spider web crystallised on bracken branch
morning skyline, light's shivering rise

A postage stamp of colour
resonates the season of the year
perfume, insect, shadow
open the landscape to the mind

Barry Granger

BEATITUDE

On the first day of March
I take my mother out to the garden.
The tall maple is bare of leaves;
I remember their shape, their shade.

Now, as she wakes, her eyes
open to the blues and greens,
the patterned body of the tree, its fractal branches,

I look only at her, feeding on signs of life
in her eyes, the lifted alertness of her face;
as brief, as sudden as the shimmering back
of a kingfisher.

Claire Coleman

FOREST MERE

I am oiling all my senses, trying
to ease the stiffness of winter.

Birds land on the wide lake below,
scissor its surface, trail chevron ripples.

Geese guard the rushes, give hard
guttural cries when I go near.

The scent of spent daffodils hangs on the air;
the fine hair of birch trees is misting with green.

I pick a small twig, touch the roughness
of a catkin patterned like snakeskin.

Its bright tuft of leaf has unfolded,
is moving, like me, towards the sun.

Rosalie Challis

APRIL, STRATFORD-ON-AVON

First foot-ferry of the year
he says,
cranking chain in the flat hull;
heaves his passenger
across this small rubicon
of north bank
to civic south.

The river splits
the frost in spring
exuberance.

Last dark twigs
hang back over the water.
Perhaps they hide
from this sharp imperative,
the cracking apart
of fly-paper buds,
the unstoppable opening of hands.

Zanna Beswick

SPRING

Pollen of willow and yew hazes the air.
In the first flush, young rush
of stubble-free spring
love explores.
Soft cheeks pillowed together,
tentative murmurs in
unbroken voices
jumbling promises with desire,
fanning the fire till
Beltane blasts in
rocking the beds,
setting the red blood coursing,
hare on hare.

Hanging on full ribbons of colour
pleated and plaited, bound unbound,
then dizzily bound again around the maypole
the dancers weave, then leave,
to lie in couples separately.
Under cover of picnicking
young loves wander to the woods,
their idle footsteps hastening.
Dusky bluebells strike the action.
In the not yet long grass barely hidden flesh flashes,
and over in secluded lay-bys
cars rock on carbon-free journeys.

Linda Perry

ROOM

This room is mine so full of light
as in the west the sun now sets,
yet still at dusk it stays so bright
a glowing warmth through windows' nets.
The window admits sound, smell
of lilacs sweet and fresh-cut grass
which father mows so all is well.
I lie abed and know all this must pass.

And though some sixty years are gone
my eye remembers yet the room.
The house is sold and we move on.
I ask: Do lilacs still the air perfume
now father mows the lawn no more
nor whistles coming through the door?

Beryl Kellow

BORDERS

Flowers and weeds tangle where a wild garden
spills into a narrow lane.

In the distance, the rattle of a speeding train.
A buzzard flies across the sky in silence.

The stone house, mellow, resting in the afternoon,
knows how this plays out year after year.

A couple, just moved in, sit reading.
Relaxing, yet anxious in their ignorance.

Trees surround them, steal rays from the evening sun,
cast shadows on their books and wineglasses.

A wooden seat, carved between two oaks
on the slope above, beckons them to its shade.

Dusk falls. He goes in. She waits till dark
to see if the animals will come.

Stephanie Boxall

TWENTY SEVEN

It's not the unremembered days you lose:
like pearls flung wide on Stinson Beach, LA
memories too are buried in the blues.

Memories get fainter every time they're used:
a picnic basket, wine, a punt in May...
it's not the unremembered days you lose.

In Girton library you kick off your shoes
with air guitar you 'get down on your knees and pray'
and now your hopes are buried in the blues.

Midnight lying together, shipping news,
Sailing By the lullaby we play:
it's not the unremembered days you lose.

Music on the terrace, taking turns to choose,
the firework-startled pheasants fly away,
a New Year promise buried in the blues.

Your brown eyes search out mine, you've paid your dues:
your strength is gone, you know you cannot stay.
It's not the unremembered days you lose
when they, like you, lie buried in the blues.

Elinor Brooks

PATRICK WALKING

Here, where grass grows lush,
where Bristol onions fringe
the trunks of trees in leaf,
dogs exercise their owners,
swifts wheel through blue skies,
is where we came six-legged
in winter. You gripping crutches,
lurching through the snow,
hot with effort, each day aiming
for another bush, a further bench,
me swaddled in thick layers,
crowned by that hideous pink hat,
cold to the bone, marvelling.

Pameli Benham

WILD STRAWBERRIES

I don't remember who said it
though I think it was one of the poets
that the slab by the tomb inscribed Entrance
should read Exit.

I considered begging to differ.
Instead I slipped

six of the sweet red berries that were clambering
over the canon's grave
into my mouth.

Deborah Harvey

2

A Touch of the Wild
Linda Saunders

... 'fox,' I whispered, 'fox'...
... as if to name it were enough
to have everything back in place, the hedgerows,
immanence, survival, the eternal laws.
John F Deane, *A Real Presence*

'Very few people', observed Robert Bly, 'are in touch with a primitive source of wildness inside them.' Just so, but an unexpected encounter with the animal world can touch a neglected wildness in all of us, waking up our senses and 'primitive' emotions of wonder or fear. For the poet, such a meeting may occasion the breakthrough of inspiration that defies conventional thought and jaded vision. A little wild epiphany occurs, 'a sudden sharp hot stink of fox', which for Ted Hughes is also the arrival of the poem itself.

Among the creatures appearing to our poets here, only one speaks in the first person out of his own world, yet ironically is the least wild and most tellingly human in our sample. Monsieur Loti's Cat, who sits as frontispiece to this section, for all his travelled sophistication of language, remains untamed: he speaks for the selfhood of all creatures, content 'just to be myself'. He guards the wild kingdom whose autonomy, however imaginative our reach, we can never fully enter. At most, longing and fearful, we conceive of a world without us, that of the Arctic Hare's 'frozen shore', or to which The Seahorses may come beyond the end of human time, 'without intention', into the renewed 'clean pastures of the sea'.

In between these 'dawn' realms, which begin and end this selection, all kinds of meetings and feelings will surprise the reader. Some stop the poet literally in her tracks, bringing a car to a standstill, as do the 'moon-snared' badgers (significantly hailed as 'Muses') in Driving John Home. A head-on encounter in Adagio for Honda and Cattle slows and quiets the world to the herd's ruminative pace, and the subtle natural sounds – 'Lark song. A bumble bee' – that speed and engine noise have excluded. A sharpened sensual and instinctual response to atmosphere, weather, season and passing time is triggered by such encounters. In their precision and strangeness, they can visit the poet like an Annunciation – the jewel-like butterfly at Jill Sharp's window; the blackbird's 'bright nib' that 'writes white on the grey air' in Dark Bullet Blackbird. They can also sensitise the mind to its fragile relationship with the natural world, to the vulnerability both of creatures and of ourselves.

Such fragility is beautifully evoked in Fownhope by the deer appearing and reappearing 'in a ghostly dance', and rumours in the pub of a cull. It is just a step to Heidi Beck's 'shame' in Mute, as she makes the connection between her fear of the swan and 'the baggage of compromised men' that the bird carries, 'rape / and the fall of Troy'. Just a further step, then, to Susan Utting's Fear of Horses, traced back from racecourses to fairgrounds to the child who saw a horse put down at a 'County Do', 'its white blaze blazed with red'.

With humour, curiosity, empathy, these poets watch, explore and take (sometimes disturbing) lessons from the otherness of creatures. Susan Jane Sims in The Kill realises the difference between animal and human killings, however vicious the former may seem:

> *It's the covering of tracks*
> *the washing of hands*
> *the desire to be clean again*
> *that marks out a human kill.*

But observation of animals may also restore a sense of innocence and connection with a more rooted, primordial and timeless way of being. Chrissy Banks in Young Again watches the mother whale gliding 'under the world of the boat', then her back emerging

> *moment by moment*
> *mile by mile*
> *like a planet*
> *swimming itself*
> *through the birthing waters*
> *back when time itself*
> *was a child.*

MONSIEUR LOTI'S CAT

Henri Rousseau's painting
of a French writer and his cat

What a comedian, what a dandy
this Monsieur Pierre Loti –
he had my round red cushion
made expressly to match his hat.

He used to leave me behind
when he went on his adventures
but now it is my turn to see the world
and where I go, he has to go –
Jerusalem, Paris, London, Washington –
he no longer has the choice.

And everywhere they ask the same questions –
who is that odd-looking, self-important man?
what on earth is he doing in that wonderful picture?
can anyone remember what was he famous for?

Monsieur Pierre wanted to be remembered
for his literary achievements
but I don't need to be remembered
because here I am.
It is enough achievement for me
just to be myself
on my ridiculous round red cushion
the ultimate full-frontally famous cat.

Monsieur Rousseau made a very good job of me –
you could run your fingers through my belly-fur
if they would let you. They won't.
We are insured for ten million euros.
Even my lovely white ears are out of bounds.

Sue Boyle

ARCTIC HARE

Lepus arcticus

Breath of the north wind
lights the sky.
Below, the arctic hare,
paws hoared with frost,
steps white-breathed on the tundra
to dig for willow twigs in the snow.
Salt-water laps the frozen shore.

Nikki Kenna

ANNUNCIATION

I was reading when he came:
a wind in my ears, then wings
of jet inlaid with rubies.

Poised on the curtain, he opened
the dark leaves, their bluish edge
soft to my touch.

On the ledge where the paint's cracked
he knelt for days,
wings clasped,

a pinch of velvet
cloistered
among bottles,

a face at the window.
Frost blessed his head on the glass,
his tiny breath.

By the solstice he lay open,
a frail Rosetta, wings
brittle as embers

blazing against the snow.

Jill Sharp

DRIVING JOHN HOME

If we'd set out with intent,
licked a finger, held it up to tell
which way the equinoctial wind was blowing,
hunkered under midnight's coats
out of range of those long
preternaturally sensitive snouts

If we'd adopted some disguise,
engaged the complicity of trees,
my hair dishevelled, snagged on twigs,
the cap you'd have donned
to stymie moonshine
wreathed with ghosts of broken leaves

If we'd watched a warrior tribe
creep circumspectly from its sett,
rootling for worms in fern
and raking grubs from bark with iron claws,
that encounter couldn't have been
any more extraordinary

than our glimpse of badgers
momentarily frozen to the tarmacadam
of Parry's Lane,
who trot into view
when I close my eyes,
fossick through my dreams.

I should not be astounded.
Brocks are native to these parts,
their pads remember lost, obliterated tracks.
Yet in that instant, with angelic serendipity,
they were moon-snared Muses
excavating poetry.

Deborah Harvey

ADAGIO FOR HONDA AND CATTLE

We meet head-on in a narrow lane
and stop the bike to let them pass.
Switch off the engine. Lark-song. A bumble-bee.
Soft patter of hooves. The world moves at their pace.
They lurch and lumber, lugging heavy bags,
swish flies and snatch mouthfuls of grass.
Behind them the white-face bull,
all maleness and muscular grace,
sleek-suited, light on his feet,
swings his brown purse.

Ama Bolton

WAITING FOR A CHANGE

Say it's late February
and we're outside on the bench,
all pulled in
against the Atlantic heave,
the meanness of an ice-pick wind,
looking down the stretch of mist,
the smudge of hill
and valley,
looking to where
land stirs against the sea.

What we're waiting for
is a chink,
the wink of a watery sun,
dance flies
starting a spring-time set,
the risky plunge
of a serotine bat
into the dark chill,
first stirrings of
a queen wasp.

Sara Butler

DARK BULLET BLACKBIRD

Wing-slick weight without resistance
other than the rain-wet air –
it's gone before I know it,
on and on, to the static tree
at the field's edge. It is lost to me
until a beaked song reaches back
across the blunt grasses,
coming over the soaked ground
and everywhere the bright nib
of whatever gave it living
writes white on the grey air
of the Spring morning.

Leanda Senior

DUSK

disturbing the ducks
gathering on the river bank
settling for the night

two drakes chasing each other
chastising the group
clustered for comfort

a duck stretches her wings
as though yawning
it is turning cold now

after the warmest October
All Hallow's E'en
this must have meaning

the sky is grey shot
with orange and a
fading blue

I will miss you
turn the other way
lean on the gate to the orchard

the sweet trees' trunks
are home for fruit flies
their sudden buzz startling me

the wren is turning in
at the far end a crow
turns to enter the hedgerow

two blue tits whisk away
know it is November
this strange turning

a golden leaf floats downstream
another one tumbling
over the changing levels

Morag Kiziewicz

AUGUST PASTORAL

Pheasant in the vegetable patch:
all summer I've seen him
reap weeds, peas, beans,
as he steps carefully between
the half-tended treasures,
his russet exotic, trail-tailed, wary.
Always with him, the dun female leads
their brood of three (fourth fox-felled)
who fade, liquid fawn, into earth
at any threat –
his colour the only defiance.

Now he struts ginger-sure,
but solitary, towards precious blueberries
while I remain careless of produce –
watching, waiting, praying
that his husbandry
proves better than mine.

Zanna Beswick

FOWNHOPE

Deer inhabit the orchard like wraiths in a churchyard.
From the cottage window I mark their movements.
At dawn, in the near left corner, they're close to the garden fence,
by mid-morning, up the slope, at wood's edge.
Come noon, in this period of April heat,
they're under the shady central clump of apple trees.
There seems no urgency in their lives, all fifteen
move in a ghostly dance, sometimes grazing,
sometimes asleep, sometimes staring at nothing,
twitching their tails; always one or two
on watch, always distant.

At the pub, we hear low-voiced rumours of a cull,
come back near midnight, a little tipsy.
Out of the car, we're compelled to stand still,
under the spell of moon, wheeling galaxies,
the urgent call of owls, scent of crushed marjoram at our feet.
With torches trained on the orchard slopes,
we find the deer clustered around a fallen tree;
their eyes return our beams. We switch off,
our breath for once slowed to theirs,
share this moment of chill night air.

Turning in through the cottage porch,
we smile at each other; small sighs of relief the only sound.
Reassured, for now, we go quietly up
the creaky stairs to bed.

Sue Chadd

THE KILL

for Emily Dickinson

The surprise is
that we are shocked
at the viciousness of the kill

and the coolness
of the killer
after the act.

Watch the lioness at rest
the satiated sleep
the playful cuff of a cub's head
the carefully retracted claws.

Rewind:
watch the lady pinpoint her target,
stalk, and strike.

It's the covering of tracks
the washing of hands
the desire to be clean again
that marks out a human kill.

And it's in the aftermath of rage
that we spot hope's feathered edges
and reach.

Susan Jane Sims

DEAD SHEEP AND CROWS

They came on tar-black wings
from messy nests of twigs,
their hungry chicks gaping.

These lazy scavengers
do not hunt, they kill.
Eat the ready dead.
Take as opportunity offers.

They came with caw, croak,
in glossy plumes, these undertakers
of the sky. To feast on
the innocent lamb
                 unseeing
                     unfeeling
                         undone.
Carry on
      carrion.
             Carry on.

Beryl Kellow

THE FEAR OF HORSES

It is the coiled spring of them before the off, reined in
and difficult against the stall, the gate, the starter's orders;

the way they twitch, their anorexic legs, that nervous
tiptoe dance they do before the ricochet of hoof on turf;

it's their eyes – scared, thyroid-startled, wanting
lids against the flies and blinkers for the crowds.

It's the queasy painted ones that whirligig
on twisted poles: precarious, gaudy, kitsch,

the dappled dobbins, hand-hewn smooth, tight-reined
Victoriana rocking on and on and getting nowhere.

It is the day a small girl took against a hobby horse,
the glassy eyes, the hoary mane, its ugly, too real face.

It is a freeze-frame scene one summer at a County Do
and being told, too late, to *come away, don't look at it* –

the useless, broken-legged thing, its white blaze
blazed with red.

Susan Utting

MUTE

I see him white, powerful, and aggressive
despite the delicate arc of his elegant neck,
the nonchalant glide through dark water.
My child reaches out from the bank
and I yank her from the strike of heavy beak,
the surge of thrusting wings, the grunt and hiss
that never come.

I have taught my child to fear
cygnus, Schwan, hakuchou, kýknos,
the swan, who arrived here before us, beating the air
over the seabed that rose to form the Himalayas.
He now bears the baggage of compromised men –
entwined with nudes, implicated in rape
and the fall of Troy, borrowed to house fey spirits,
the grief of love, the despair of our dying.

The swan dips his head, nibbles a weed, and I am shame,
but that does not concern him either.

Heidi Beck

WOODLOUSE

So hard to like in your dogged determination
to explore my room.
You're not a communicator,
just a waver of legs.
You're only sort of black, neither are you glossy,
there's no shine to your character.
Dull. Just a dull wanderer
sniffing or feeling or probably just
vaguely sensing damp stuff.
Your patterned back, again ordinary,
just a few stripes in different
tones of muted plainness.

Little creature, little paradox,
is it your ordinariness that makes you unique?

David Cohen

WORM

Slippery squiggly wiggly worm,
tireless friend of gardeners,
chunky spaghetti for blackbirds and robins,
a reliable muncher making mulch,
chomping through leaf mould to your
elongated heart's delight.
Oh how you love the words
Dust to dust, ashes to ashes – it's your menu.
Marvell's threat is a promise for you
and you deserve it –
for all your patient masticating
through rotting veggies, decaying plants,
legs, arms, heads, ears, eyes and the lovely bits.
No difference to you though, they're all lovely bits.

Semi-transparent bendy pencil
you dive dive dive to escape the ravening beak and
the indiscriminate spade,
to return to your subterranean catacombs
and play knotting games as you wind
yourselves together in the
freedom of the soil.

David Cohen

THE CANVAS OF MY BRAIN

Biology at school was a boring
catalogue of names:
the parts of a flower,
bones in the body,
species of fish.
Words were knives used
to dissect a corpse
in a search for the secrets of life.

Once an old priest took me bird-watching
along the cliffs of St. Bees:
cormorants, shags,
guillemots and terns,
numerous varieties of gull,
and many whose names
I cannot recall. Briefly,
I felt the passion in those lists.

When my grandmother died, I found
my grandfather's 'Sketch-Book
of British Birds', covered in brown
paper and dated 1898.
My eyes were enchanted
by the artist's depiction of texture
and tone, the subtle gradations
of colour down a duck's back.

Yesterday, for the first time I looked
at a lobster out of water, living
but doomed on a fishmonger's slab, claws
bound by thick beige rubber bands;
for the first time I saw
with an artist's attention, and was awed
by its indigo shell
and tail fringe of orange hairs.

Eagerly, I stared at cream nodules
near the claws and the various
pinks on its segmented underside.
I wanted to paint
the creature on the canvas
of my brain. But already
the colours have run,
the outline is blurred.

Today, as I rest on green turf above grey
cliffs and look down hundreds of feet
to the grizzled sea, I am practising my art;
trying to sketch the exact
tints of grey on my mind's
future, to etch in my memory
the two great black-backed gulls
riding thermals above my head.

Jeremy Young

ROCK POOL

Imagine a sea snail, how it feels its track like a finger
drawn softly over the sandy base of a rock pool, its emergence
from brine to breeze, wobbling slightly like a slow stone on a mission;
what is it like to wait for the waves and then let go,
tumbling into the tidal force with such reckless release
from trails of safety?

Imagine a crab, feeling itself secure and secreted –
then netted; how does it cope with capture, being plucked
from the known world, with all its variation and scope, confined
in a bucket with no fathoming the scoop
from freedom to this inhospitable exile,
that looming human face?

Claire Coleman

YOUR AGAIN

As if they'd been waiting for us,
they appear,

their black backs two wet rocks
that have learnt to swim.

Show-offs, mother and baby.
Snorting fountains, they glide,
buck and dip,
play us
with their vanishing acts –

and *there!*
re-appear upended,
cleft tails raised till,
toppling,

a weight of leather
slaps against the ocean's skin.

Then the mother whale glides
under the world of the boat.
And we are young again,
bums up, leaning over the side,
to witness the slow slide
of her back
emerging.
And it keeps coming,
moment by moment,
mile by mile,
like a planet
swimming itself
through the birthing waters
back when time itself
was a child.

Chrissy Banks

LANYON QUOIT

Under the granite capstone
horses plash in mud,
dredge puddled water.

Blown here by hurricane rumours,
by winds,
they kiss each other's necks

nibble, nudge, bare teeth
passing each other's shoulders;
eyes roll, ears prick.

The wind has tattered their manes.
In the sour, spiked grass
hard platforms of cobbled dung.

They have sheltered here for centuries
since long before the storm
that brought the dolmen

to its knees and broke one leg.
Its roof is lower now,
the horses' backs are bare.

Once there were riders;
once they were ridden there.

Elinor Brooks

THE SEAHORSES

after Edwin Muir

After the seven hundred years
that will put the world to sleep
let it be the turn of the seahorses
to drift through pale chambers
sculpted by thorny spines,
grazing on seeds of quartz, riding
the coral currents of the earth's slow heart.

Let their sonic poems be its lullaby,
their tails lyres, fashioned to make music
from a tide drawn behind a darkling moon.
In place of heralds singing the first dawn,
only a lifting of their equine heads,
a stillness in the herd to mark the warmth
stirring an almost-barren deep.

And let there be light, to show the slow
undoing of darkness made by the lost,
two-legged race. May the seahorses come
without intention, no urge to help repeat
what came to be. This time around, no
heart-piercing servitude;
only the bright, clean pastures of the sea.

Louise Green

3

As if the Sea
Rosie Jackson

Water has always had an incredible power to burst the lines of the literal and move us into the world of myth and metaphor. The opening poem in this section, Louise Green's Here, reminds us that water lives 'below the surface of everything / that it will run through your dreams'. Water lies in our bodies, our blood, our memories. As something too big for us to contain, it is often linked with the unconscious, with what lies beyond our rational knowing. So in Elinor Brooks' St Ives, 'Dreams swim deep into / midnight's harbour', and in Sue Boyle's Candles for the Kursk, Vasily is 'afraid in a deeper sleep / he might dream again / the black, the mass / and patience of that water'.

The sea delivers us to an underworld full fathom five, where everything is new and strange. In these poems, water changes everything: it defines landscapes, shapes perception, determines life and death. Sue Chadd's poem Aldeburgh, Suffolk, features Maggi Hambling's magnificent sculpture on Aldeburgh beach – *Scallop* – part of an artist's dialogue with the ocean, intended to evoke 'the mysterious power of the sea'. And this whole section can be read as a series of writers' conversations with the sea, with water in its many protean forms: mist, ice, rain, well, stream, lake, leat, river, flood, wave, tide, ocean. Sometimes the voice is grateful and lyrical, celebrating the way water induces feelings of freedom, spaciousness and beauty. Elsewhere the tone is reflective, wary, aware of the depths beneath the surface.

We have here literal places by the sea: the rich sparseness of Orkney, a windswept Suffolk, Dorset's sweeping Chesil Beach, the resort of St Ives and the wildness of Polurrian Bay in Cornwall, an evocative Tea Tree Lake on the Tyagarah Nature Reserve in New South Wales, Crescent Beach in Western Canada. We have creatures found in or near the sea: fulmar, curlew, dolphin, whale, pilchard, mussel. And on the edge of the sea we have a liminal world that is neither land nor water, a place where earth ends, where things dissolve and are transformed, as in Jay Arr's Breaking the Night: 'At the edge no boundaries: / pebbles, sea, sky, stars merge'. Over half the poems in this section are set where the elements of earth and water meet –beaches, seaside towns, coastal walks, places whose very landscape is determined by their nearness to the sea – shingle, sand, salt air, reeds, mallow, marram grass. This is where the known and named give way to the unknown, the limitless.

The sea has always had this resonance with the unboundaried and is often used figuratively in poetry to intimate all that lies beyond human understanding and power. Norfolk poet Jay Appleton calls his coastal landscape an 'encounter with infinity'. Emily Dickinson, in her poem As if the Sea should part, imagines the sea opening to show another sea, then another, the receding watery vision opening indefinitely. But if the ocean is a metaphor for the infinite and timeless (Jacques Cousteau calls it 'the great unifier, man's only hope'), it also shows up by contrast our human frailty and vulnerability. Water is indispensable to life but can also be the instrument of death. There are not many people in these poems: water has taken over, shaped the landscape, immersed us in its element, left us changed or drowned.

This ominous role of the sea runs as an implied undercurrent through much of this section to become explicit in three of the final poems. In the deceptively simple Heavy Rain, Stewart Carswell uses a taut final metaphor to suggest the equal drowning of trees and people, his river as implacable as Eliot's in *Four Quartets*, 'destroyer, reminder / Of what men choose to forget'. The Titanic disaster of 14 April 1912 is never actually named in Leanda Senior's Unbelievable, but her original slant ingeniously reverses the events of that night when 1,500 lives were lost, lifting us back to a moment of eternity untouched by tragedy, 'a place where it didn't happen'. Sue Boyle's restrained elegy Candles for the Kursk is a moving tribute to those who died aboard the Russian nuclear submarine Kursk in the Barents Sea on 12 August 2000. But what these poems capture is the human pulse behind these stories, the beat of personal history and experience, 'the mystery, terrors, blisspoints' of their years.

Along the top rim of Maggi Hambling's four-metre-high steel scallop shells at Aldeburgh are incised some words from Britten's opera Peter Grimes: 'I hear those voices that will not be drowned'. These are the voices in this section: voices of celebration, interrogation, love, memory, reflection, elegy, wonder. The final poem, Sue Chadd's tightly crafted The Mirror Ship, transforms the remains of a shipwreck into an affirmation of life: 'I have made it from your death song'. This is the power of poetry: to refuse to be silenced, even in the face of loss and tragedy; to make words themselves do what the sea does and wash things anew.

HERE

The coldest, wettest, snowiest parish in the county
the guide book tells you. Freezing fog
doesn't get a mention, the sort that
has you lost in your own back garden
or how in winter the hills bare all,
hidden water leaping into view
silver as a salmon's back
coursing down limestone leats,
the canopy of Limekiln Woods
a clean rib-cage dripping melted ice
into the mossy chamber of St Dunstan's Well
where the water-meadows of Alder Grove
turn to sheets of gold in a low sun and
dawn mists thick as milk have the cattle
standing like land-locked ships.

It doesn't tell you water has a way
of turning on you, that people remember
prayer books floating down the aisle,
dogs swept into slockers, cavers
lost to flash floods,
rivers entering by back doors
leaving by the front,
that water calls to water here, rain
torrenting into millstreams, forming
inland breakers, drowning calves
and sheep; how water lives
below the surface of everything,
that it will run through your dreams.

Perhaps they want to lull you
into thinking this is a kind country,
the sort it might be possible
to turn your back on.
It isn't. You can't.
This is a place that threads itself
through you, traps you
into a sort of love called *here*,
strikes like a fist
in that place you call your soul.

Louise Green

ALDEBURGH, SUFFOLK

for Benjamin Britten and Maggi Hambling

Water snakes through reeds and grasses
in a hot flood, crowding mallow stalks, whitening
summer's shadow to a place of bones.
Walking the shingle has never been harder,
and the sea wind takes your words, your song
from my mouth, flinging them in a red horse canter
around metal scallop shells, to Thorpeness, to Sizewell.
Now the quiet season has almost come again.
Ripe pears hang in sunlight, just out of reach.

Sue Chadd

ORKNEY: KETTLETOFT TO QUOYNESS

Sunday: the square deserted
the pub closed

three fishing boats
tethered at the pier

a portacabin bank
(open on Tuesdays)

an empty road
between level barley-fields

a fulmar on its nest
in the ruins of a church

a meadow of yellow iris
where sheep and gravestones sleep

shimmer of marram
under the midsummer sky

curlew rolling its name
purely purely over the silence

a long walk on a ridge of sand
between back-to-back bays

the cairn's open eye
looks east across the sea

Ama Bolton

TEA TREE LAKE

Single file we arrive
at this surprise of water.
Melaleuca alternifolia surrounds us.
The Australian sun sweats
oils from the trees.
The burning day softens,
the lake is warm as a womb.
Calm descends, moon rises
on dispersed swimmers,
the only sound
my body's slow movement.
Naked, unafraid of unreached depths,
I am making a memory:
balm in the years to come.

Claire Coleman

CRESCENT BEACH

On Crescent Beach, Pacific waters reach
From Western Canada toward Japan
And dolphins, trusting, leap into my mind.
On Crescent Beach the shoulder of the day
Slopes gently down towards the coming night
And children play, such innocent delight.
The bags are packed. We silently alone
Give thanks for friendship in this lovely place
And drive the highway to the plane for home.
The mind a garden, filled to our delight
And we, refreshed, are ready to go on
To all that we have known when we are home.
Night falls; above the clouds, we slowly fly.
Its darkness touches that deserted beach,
Our memories brushwood on the rising tide.

Ewan A MacPherson

FLORES ISLAND, BRITISH COLUMBIA

Salty air, cool on my cheek, stings me awake
as we walk down the wooden path to the boat.

Life jackets on, we start her up, leave the inlet,
the safety of the cloud-forest mountains,
steer into open water.

Sea and sky spread out before us
as we set a course for the feeding grounds.
I breathe in the smell of freedom, give
myself up to the rocking of the boat.

Evening. In the firelight, survival suits
swing gently from the rafters, cast
giant shadows on the walls.

We sip hot chocolate from tin mugs in silence.
In the dark and cold, whales breach and dive.

Stephanie Boxall

BREAKING THE NIGHT

The ebb's hiss is slack
playing with the beach.
I've waded out thigh-deep
night fishing Chesil's curve
beaded with sleepy lanterns
winking out above the water-mark.
At the edge no boundaries:
pebbles, sea, sky, stars merge.

Fishing's an excuse to be alone with the night.
Satellites dot-dash, alternately blotting,
blinking, out on the eighty-minute round.
An ocean's swell murmurs peace and bliss.

This is.

Suddenly the rod spasms,
tip kissing waves.
The reel screams.
Down the beach
the shout echoes

Shoal! Shoal!

Jay Arr

ST IVES

Far across the sand
and out at sea
stands a white candle: there
Godrevy's palest star
glimmers through gauzy nets
of silver-pink
and milky blue
that thicken with the dark.

Dreams swim deep into
midnight's harbour:
dorsal-finned
and dolphin-backed
packed as close as pilchards,
black as the lighthouse rock,
they surface, roll and dive,
churning sleep.

Winched by morning tide,
wave-woven cover
exposes inch by inch
the bay's wide-arcing reach;
the sea lies on its back,
watches slow-wheeling
birds descend
from the sky's high ceiling.

Elinor Brooks

ON POLURRIAN BEACH

High above us the white hotel hangs like a bird
wings outstretched for flight, coverts flexed
to skim my head should it decide upon
an uprush of thermals to glide the wild Atlantic.

Down here they ride horses through the tide
as though another journey had begun,
a lesser one, from the place where rock cracks tarmac
and the road home melts beneath our gaze.

We stand hag-ridden, like pullulating clouds
of storm and ragged weather. We are pewter
or the blue-black ink of mussels over-crowding
every niche. Though its shimmer will break

promises, we hunt the horizon's curve. Waves
slide by and suck the sand from under our feet.

Shirley Wright

HEAVY RAIN

The river, brown with victory,
claims ground and marches seaward.

Trees cling to the gorge,
taunted by the procession,

but all they can do is stare
at their reflections in the water,

watch their children drown downstream.

Stewart Carswell

UNBELIEVABLE

Even though it's happened, it's still unbelievable.
A Night to Remember, 14 April 1912

Even though the ending will always be this

there is a place where it didn't happen

where the vessel is steaming across the wide ocean
the passengers praising her resolute bulkheads
where the wireless operator is keeping
the night traffic going
and the steward is manning his station
right into the Roaring Twenties
and the perfect martini
where the architect's drawings
are constantly ship-shape
where the Latvian wheelwright is holding
his wife in the warmth of their cabin
and where two lovers are making the love
for the baby that's coming
where a village from Ireland is safe on the boat
that is taking her westwards and singing
and dancing away from the famine
like there's no tomorrow
where bells and whistles are shouting
on docksides to come see
the ship in the offing
where a man and a woman are murmuring words
the vast cup of happiness passing

between them and on from each hand to all hands

around the one long table

Leanda Senior

CANDLES FOR THE KURSK

Who knows what was lost
when the sea took charge of them?
Who knew them enough to say,
Ignore his name, his rank.
This was the man he was.

Sergei's son, the virgin Nikolai,
black-toothed and garlic-breathed –
an acrobat in Omsk once looked his way.
Unless with that speechless
airy, supple, spangled girl,
he wanted no truck with love.

Some waited hours, a few waited
days to die. When each is his own
darkness, his memory scrolling,
flickering to its end, who knows
the mystery, terrors,
blisspoints of his years?

This for Vasily, Anya's favourite son,
student of orchids, shore leave stargazer,
who laughed and drank too much
and slept too lightly,
afraid in a deeper sleep
he might dream again
the black, the mass
and patience of that water.

Sue Boyle

THE MIRROR SHIP

I am not lonely in this star garden.
I have made it from your death song,
from shipwrecked spars, flotsam, tide-line shrapnel.
Night and day mean nothing now,
but rolled stones can warm in spring light,
and your shadow is quiet here.
Although the North Sea pounds the shingle ridge,
sea kale, sea pea and feathered fennel hold hard,
grasp the centre of the earth with salted roots,
stabilise my black love, your mermaid fire.

Sue Chadd

4

What We Know about Love
Stephanie Boxall

I have taken the title for this section from Claire Dyer's poem The Day Elvis Died. In it, the narrator evokes a time defined, among other things, by 'what we didn't know about love'. Turning that line on its head seemed to me the perfect way to sum up the following group of poems, originally gathered together by the section editors under the heading Personal Relationships.

Of course, relationships don't always fall neatly within the happy confines the word love might initially suggest. But I was reminded of the story What We Talk about When We Talk about Love by the American poet and short story writer Raymond Carver, and the idea that love means different things to different people. To me the word contains all the happiness, sadness, bitterness, regret, longing, anticipation, excitement, agony and ecstasy that characterise the complex emotional contracts human beings make with one another.

Indeed, as I began to go through the section it became clear that the overriding tenor of the poems was one of sadness. Nikki Kenna's Chancing on an Exhibition and Claire Dyer's Cornish Wagon reawaken the memory of a lost love, Caroline Heaton's prose poem Reunion tenderly evokes a life that might have been, Rachael Clyne's Terminal Conversation and Rosalie Challis's Book Ends both tackle the subject of death. This sombre mood was so prevalent that the only place I could find for Louise Green's ingenious couplet, To His Coy Mistress, 1967, was here:

> *Please, Louise,* said boyfriend Will,
> *If you don't let me, I'll be ill.*

This isn't the only happy piece. Louise's poem Arrivals, a joyful celebration of birth and family life, and Linda Perry's Plums, a witty perspective on the old parlour game 'He loves me, he loves me not' take their places among the other poems in the section. But these three are rare. Claire Coleman's delicate Two Person High bridges the gap, perhaps, starting with a memory of perfect happiness and ending on a note of caution born of the wisdom of experience. And with Sara Butler's spare and haunting Sanctuary, we begin to catch a glimpse of the dark side of love.

Along with the romantic pieces are poems dealing with family life and relationships: the love of a child for a parent, for example, as in Caroline Heaton's Prospero and Daughter, containing the stunning image of the daughter as 'a pint-sized Miranda', or the powerful bonds that tie us to family and home, illustrated poignantly in Claire Dyer's The Day Elvis Died and in Sara-Jane Arbury's Cream Teas, a clever response to a poem by Jo Roach. Heidi Beck's poem Love evokes with deceptive simplicity the complex relationship between parent and child, while Chrissy Banks' The Gift offers a moving insight into a moment of tenderness between mother and son.

After the hustle and bustle, exuberance and passion of these different kinds of love, it seems logical to bring the section to a close with four poems reflecting on loss. Rachael Clyne's and Rosalie Challis's exquisitely quiet pieces home in on that awful moment when the death of a loved one is both imminent and inevitable. Clare Diprose's skilful Mourning uses the sharp, clear images of a childhood memory to bring a parent vividly to life, and Barry Granger's Open and Closed leaves us with the feeling that even though the person we have loved may have gone they are somehow always with us.

One poem, Claire Dyer's Where It Is, seems to encapsulate the whole subject of love and is the poem with which I have chosen to open the section. I believe that, in their different ways, all the poems here tell us with great beauty and skill 'what we know about love'. I like to think Raymond Carver would agree with me and I hope you will too.

WHERE IT IS

It's in the oyster hour, the one
before morning when the sky unfolds from its corners
and the air trembles with the strain of it.

It's later, in the gabble of eucalyptus leaves
and how the hydrangea outside my door
nods its heavy heads as if to say *I know*.

It's in where the sea is, all the salt spray and churn of it,
the whisk of wingtip on water – of fulmar, tern.
It's in the creak of bark, how moss scribbles its signatures on it

and it's in the silence of mountains,
from vast and scree to bee chatter
and the sound of pollen falling.

It's in the travelled hour,
the one before nightfall.
This is where love is, when the sky folds back in.

Claire Dyer

PROSPERO AND DAUGHTER

I was a pint-sized Miranda
to your bit-part Prospero, Papa –
lugging the tomes
from the lower shelves
to cradle them in my lap,
musty dolls of leather and yellow paper.

While you were at the beach
scanning the sea for ships,
irritably plucking from your ankles
the fleshy greenweed
thrown by the sea-swirl,
I snuffed up the sulphurous scent of magic,

laboured a forefinger over
the black battlements of Gothic letter
in foreign tongues.
The dark lines marched on and on,
drawing me after them
into a future I could not read.

If I could find one charm
to break the charm,
release us both
from this island of print,
to float us free –

but still your horizon-gazing figure
compels me across the years:
picking my way over the miles of seashells
and whitened stones like bones,
I scoop a handful,
tug your windtorn sleeve.

Caroline Heaton

CREAM TEAS

after Jo Roach

I come from maiden names, Miss Shipley, Miss Parker,
First Day Covers and Blue Peter badges, tea trays,
Premium Bonds, the missing of Genette Tate,
the bend in the lane, her sideways bicycle, school photo smile,
from lazy-eye patches, pennies from Schweppes
and the sister who never came.

I come from sterilising and starter bras,
Dr Whites, pierced ears, rheumatoid arthritis.
I come from dancing with my mum to the Top Forty
on a Sunday night after the ironing,
dressing-gowns and slippers,
cornflakes for supper,
the Test Card girl in the telly.

I come from whitewashed houses with small front doors,
treadmarks on the polished step.
I come from money growing on trees.
I come from the lone oak in a ploughed field.
I come from trespassers who will be prosecuted.
I come from knocked-up women and knocked-down men
who worked a land they would never own.

Sara-Jane Arbury

THE DAY ELVIS DIED

we were packing.
Already the moving vans
were a low rumble across the Severn

bringing with them the ending of our Wales,
the loss of our elderflower valley,
our precious skim of sea.

It had been a time of horses,
bottle-green school uniforms,
the boy in the coal shed, his hand

on my waist. It had been about cigarettes
and village shops, about Thursday
Youth Club and *Songs of Praise* filming

in the church. The summers had been
long and hot, winters blew in on the wind.
We'd tasted leeks, sweet after the first frost

and our house stood bright and white
above the lane to the beach.
It had been about wonderment

and what we didn't know about love:
about pocketfuls of rainbows
and crying in the chapel, suspicious

minds, and softly as I leave you,
about hearts of stone. We packed
away the radio just before the news.

Why, I asked, standing at her bedroom door,
is it wall-to-wall Elvis today?
Perhaps, my sister said, *it's his birthday.*

Claire Dyer

PLUMS

Today I picked a pot of plums
and chose those plums with care,
succulent deep, deep purple
with a velvety, sleek bloom.
I picked a pot of plums
for a bit of fun.

You know that old game:
he loves me, he loves me not, he loves me...
I cooked them long and slow,
put in a splash of red wine, too.
Got out my favourite dish with the wide rim,
perfect for balancing stones,
and I ate those sweet, sweet plums,
one by one.
He loves me, he loves me not, he loves me...

But I knew well before the end
that all my dreams would come true,
because I had learnt long ago,
avoid numbers of plums divisible by two.
One, three, five, seven all lead to heaven.
It's odd
he loves me.

Linda Perry

TWO PERSON HIGH

How he made me laugh; he did magic tricks
with his fingers, withdrew flowers
from behind my ear, then ate the petals
one by one.

We were bathed in sunlight,
played shadow-less on the beach,
practising acrobalances where the sand
was soft and nothing could hurt us.

Would I dare, now, to stand on a man's shoulders,
bend to clasp with him, hand to hand, lift
my self so my feet reach up to the sky,
turn the world up side down for love?

Claire Coleman

SANCTUARY

On the dark edge
of a village
there's an old phone box
the colour of charcoal,
lined with books.
I imagine, as one evening
life takes a turn for the worse,
a woman quick-stepping
along the lane
to its shelter,
the misty glow of a single bulb
the heavy door closing,
the way she runs her finger
up and down the spines
until the right one answers.

Sara Butler

REUNION

My other life walks beside me, the one I might have lived with you. It is at home with the Islington square, the cast-iron railings and lamppost, with the cat crossing the street at right angles. It walks between us like a shadowy child, swinging a little, evenly, on our hands; testing the weight we can bear. It is at peace with the dusk, the half-moon emerging, the woman who puts out her milk bottles, as she does every evening. At peace with the dusk, which could also be dawn, with the moon, which is either appearing or disappearing – with the pink and white geraniums against a green wooden shutter, a pink almost white, and a white with the brilliance of the moon. It teases me with your habit of walking on the kerbside, as sons were taught in the Sixties, and with your habit of quoting languages I only half understand. It is patient when I shrug away the jacket I do not need, with my silences and volubility, my unspoken nostalgia and refusals. My other life keeps step with my halts and stumbles, walks me all the way to the Angel, says goodbye affectionately and regretfully. It accompanies you home, slowly pacing your long street, curls up beside you – grieves me just enough.

Caroline Heaton

CORNISH WAGON

Museum of English Rural Life, 2012

Seeing it stops my heart the length of a word.
I thought I'd forgotten,
but, in its scarred wood, its wheels
shoulder-high and marked out

with hammer blows, his father's name
painted on a panel at the front,
is that moment after the harvest
when Joe said, *Whoa, Boy*,

and the horse stilled, the heat rising
sweet and thick from him. Mill Lane
and the Lower Field were evening,
the air above us weary, and birds

sang like needlecraft. They stitched
the sky, almost silk it was.
Not so our clothes, Joe's and mine,
rough with leftover grain.

It stuck to our skin as he kissed me,
his shirt dull with dust
and sweat from between
his shoulder blades.

We lay together when the clouds were dark
and him hard like stone.
His love afterwards
had no heat left, was what

remained, he said. It made me
remember water from the yard pump
when it has the sun in it.
And afterwards: a splinter

in my palm from the wagon-bed
that dug deep, hurt
in colour, and the child
who would bring me here

to this and you who, turning say,
Hey, let's go. So I leave,
one long look back from the door,
my hand still sore, still stinging.

Claire Dyer

CHANCING ON AN EXHIBITION

Bob Osborne, artist, born 1953,
University of East Anglia 1972–5

I push on the door
squeeze through the gap
to stand on the painted concrete
in that quiet space.
The door closes.

Nailed to the walls
collage of flotsam and jetsam
from an unknown artist.
Atlantic washed,
a Newlyn tiller, an oar,
a piece of net, knotted still,
cut loose from the fisher's boat,
and pinned.
Discarded sardine tins
frame plastic soldiers glued inside.
Palmistry prints mark rice paper.

Inside the catalogue, I see your face,
your name, the date
that you were born.

And hanging too
the print of a Porthmeor wave
with a circle
the colour of the rose
you left between the sheets
of my university bed

thirty-seven years gone.

Nikki Kenna

ARRIVALS

His was some arrival –
midnight, a thunderstorm flaying the hospital car-park
hair plastered flat, limbs candle-waxed for speed,
a tiny human cannonball aimed straight at our hearts
rugby-tackled into a cellular blanket
by a startled midwife.

He took his place
at the top of the sibling chain, first to beat a path through life,
a beacon for the others. He grew into himself,
departed first, south-bound, single,
leaving a queue of brothers
fighting for his room.

All our years a swaddle,
a huddle, a gaggle of human warmth leading up to
this January Friday – the snap of laundered sheets,
beer in the fridge, the travel-cot wiped down,
the just-can't-wait hours until we meet
his newborn daughter.

Louise Green

LOVE

I bought my daughter a *Snow White* dress
the Christmas after the divorce
though she prefers to play Rapunzel
with her long tangled hair
which I comb strand by strand.

In the afternoon when she is hungry
I offer an apple because it is healthy.
She says she cannot bite it
with her wobbly tooth and would prefer
wedges of her chocolate orange.

I cut the apple into pieces
and put them in a bowl.
She sighs and holds out her hand.

Heidi Beck

THE GIFT

After the accident, the hospital
they brought me aching home
mouth pumped up like a tyre
black stitches tracking the wound
over my lip, the red slit signalling
the broken place. And my son
my tall, cool son of sixteen
kissed the top of my head
and over the curve of my shoulder
laid his arm, like the broad wing
of a mother bird guarding its young.

Anyone who has known tenderness
thrown like a lifeline into the heart of pain
anyone who has known pain bleed into tenderness
knows how the power of the two combine.
And if I am a fool to give thanks
for pain as well as tenderness
and even if, as some would say
there are no accidents

still, I am grateful for the gift.

Chrissy Banks

BOOK ENDS

She has done this before, Betty,
listened to her sister's failing breath,
fading like the afternoon light,
but I am a stranger to dying.

Betty and I sit stiff on upright chairs,
facing each other, not seeing,
my mother on the bed between.

Rosalie Challis

TERMINAL CONVERSATION

What can we talk about when
events in the rest of the house
no longer hold meaning

when tomorrow really is
a singular possibility
and the outside world
or any future stops
at this room?

What can I say when
everything I mention
points to your departure?

Tending your body
bathing in silence together:

the only conversation left.

Rachael Clyne

MOURNING

I am eight again, and face my mother.
We grasp the corners of a sheet,
flick, crack and stretch white cotton
between us, match and straighten edges,
and walk to meet each other.

She passes me her corners,
slides her hands down, picks up the fold.
We back away until the fabric is taut,
begin again. Dance it over and over.

What's left of the sun
slides down below the roof
and winter cabbages are shadowed with blue.
I fold cool pillowcases from the line,
drop inherited clothes-pegs
into my basket, one by one.
Low over the darkening hedge drifts
a pale nightdressed owl.

Clare Diprose

OPEN AND CLOSED

Bedroom: a watershed in my life,
bed, cosy, warmth, drifting, together.
The moment is all
touch, affection, dignity, love,
time standing still, holding out, letting go.
The presence, the scent of Dad,
the man gone,
the spirit here.

Horizon: playing fields, the pitch,
unshackled, engaging, together.
Man, boy; father, son. Time never ending,
playing, learning, growing, holding hands,
safe, protected, secure, loved.
The presence, the scent of Dad,
the man everlasting,
the man here.

Barry Granger

5

Connected Elsewhere
Ama Bolton

People arouse our curiosity. They are the focus of powerful emotions. Some, like the mesmerising Jimmy in Sara Butler's Rhythm, inspire adoration. Others, like the man in Deborah Harvey's powerfully understated poem His Father provoke rage. We find people fascinating because through observing them we can learn about ourselves. We compare and contrast. We find out who we are, and what we are not, in the mirror of those around us.

Few things can be more mysterious than the mind of another person. Each of us has a unique back-story, possesses an idiosyncratic range of inherited or acquired strengths and weaknesses, and develops an individual template for seeing and responding to the world. We do have much in common, of course, but it is a wonder to me that we can communicate, given all our differences. Even our most intimate friends and family are capable of astonishing us, while a chance encounter with a stranger, such as that in Heidi Beck's quietly observant poem In a Coffee House in Bath can overwhelm us with sympathy.

Interest in our fellow men and women is responsible for sublime works of literature as well as the shameful excesses of gutter journalism. The common obsession with celebrities is perhaps not due to curiosity alone, but to the basest manifestation of the religious impulse: we need gods so badly that we may be driven to look for them in the strangest of temples or to create them from dust. Two of the poems that follow, It's a Dog's Life by Ray Fussell and An Audience with Dirk by Jill Sharp, show contrasting examples of latter-day deities, delineated with few words, but just the right ones.

Each of us lives at the centre of a many-layered web of connections: family, work, shared interest, home town, home team, nation. At each level there is potential for misery or joy: sibling rivalry or sisterly love, xenophobia or passionate philanthropy. All this is rich matter for poetry. Barry Granger's Twickenham is a muscular, masculine poem of gutsy solidarity. Deborah Harvey's poem gives a glimpse of family loyalties under strain, while the story in Pameli Benham's Beginning is told with such care and good humour that one feels optimistic about these honeymooners. Human figures can give focus to a landscape, and meaning to an interior, as in Sue Chadd's subtly witty poem of non-communication, The Visit. Just as a live model is the most challenging subject for the artist, so the subject of our fellow human beings makes the greatest demands on our resources as writers. All our instincts are sharpened as we attempt to make sense of them, and consequently of ourselves.

In both Zanna Beswick's Fish Auction and Clare Diprose's At the City Institute you will find deep humanity and meticulous attention to detail combined with a strongly individual imagination. Sue Boyle's The Evensong and Pameli Benham's Remember This tell their stories with clear-eyed compassion. In every piece there is the economy of expression that so often distinguishes poetry from prose. Look at the poem that rounds off this section, Reading Mandelstam by Caroline Heaton: not a syllable is wasted.

I have grown to love these poems for their truth and beauty as well as for the sense of connection they give me. I am sure you, too, will find something of yourself in them.

RHYTHM

First time I see
Jimmy
I think he's an angel
up on the back of a trailer,
hair like barley straw
evening sun coming low
through the trees
giving him a halo.

I squint up at him
from the barn floor
and him, he's like a
pendulum
swinging his body from
side to side,
lifting the bales
one by one
one by one
pitching them down
to the men below.

This rhythm,
he says,
it gets a hold of you
and it stays.

Me, I think
I'd like a bit of that
rhythm too.

Sara Butler

AT THE CITY INSTITUTE

Behind spiked railings, two jackdaws
and a pigeon stroll on worn grass.
From bare plane trees, fruit dangles –
Christmas baubles left up too long.

Attendant litter bins wait beside seats.
The new bike rack stands empty.
Queues of stoic chimneys line up
above rows of sash windows

and door after solid door. This one
asks to be opened, a pop-up book
of tall rooms and sea-grey carpet
leading up imposing stairs to where

loose-limbed and a bit rumpled,
Bob watches from his portrait,
long fingers curled round a cup
of the refreshments he provides,

other skills being harder to depict.
His chair edges onto a magic carpet
from which he accomplishes
ordinary astonishments of care.

Behind him, skewing perspective,
stretches the fossil cast that draws him
here, and out from this building to swim
through sharp-toothed Jurassic seas

where this vast creature with one stroke
of its wrongly positioned flippers
glides past him, its nod of gratitude
for all the dusting just perceptible.

Clare Diprose

IN A COFFEE HOUSE IN BATH

The girl in the soft chair has miraculous fingers
tapping swift semaphore across the tablet in her lap.
On the sofa a couple debates in a foreign language,
waving and jabbing their mobile phones.

The man at the table on the left communes with his Guardian
while the man on the right scowls at the Telegraph crossword,
their phones poised on their tables like duelling guns.

Over there, next to the window and the world outside
a woman wipes her eyes with a wad of white tissue,
pushing it up under glasses with thick black frames.
There is devastation somewhere.

I almost move to comfort her,
but her gaze never once leaves the screen
of the slender laptop in front of her.
Her ears are plugged and wired
to sounds I cannot hear.

She must be all right, I suppose,
here where we've gathered to share
the fact that we're all connected elsewhere.

Heidi Beck

REMEMBER THIS

Remember this. She no longer can.
In A & E they probe and she sits dumb,
lifts her empty eyes towards their faces,
lets their questions trickle through her mind
leaving no sense of what they ask, no clue
to what they need to know, traps tight
the memories that made her who she is.

Does she know her name? Are there people
running through the streets, wild with worry,
shouting out her name? What do they call?
Sometimes, in her head, she hears her mother
singing *Feigele, my little bird*,
promising her strawberries, new shoes,
but she stays hiding in the silver birches.

Firmly the nurses prise her handbag from her,
ease the grip of grubby, jewelled fingers,
and see it stuffed with crumpled bits of paper,
flyers, tickets, faded scraps of newsprint.
They find no letters, diary, photographs,
and miss the meaning of her stolen bread,
food to appease the memory of hunger.

Pameli Benham

AN AUDIENCE WITH DIRK

Home at last from the Riviera, knowing
he must not look back

he walks Knightsbridge in dark chapeau
and shades. The grey light hurts.

At night, rehearsing his own lines –
memoir, novels – he is word

perfect. After the performance
a hushed procession wends

towards him and each advancing celebrant
drops their gaze,

suddenly shy to lay before him
their unread offering. One swift flourish

and he's marked the pristine page
with a blue-black emblem,

raising his head, briefly, to show those
eyes.

The people find him gracious; but gods,
when they grow old, crave

adoration. How else are they to know
if there are still believers?

Jill Sharp

IT'S A DOG'S LIFE

I envy your tenacity, Brian Moore:

you were the Harlequin hooker
who played for England,
ears bandaged against your head
to preserve your ugliness,
chest out for the anthem.

Rugby was your pathological
passion, your licence to harm
and be harmed.
Built like an illegal pit bull,
your bite unending
till molar met molar.

Intellect forgives parents,
adopters and teachers,
but your heart still rages.

It took six years of benders,
three marriages and two daughters
to temper your temper.

Ray Fussell

TWICKENHAM

Crescendo: colour, passion
Land of Hope and Glory
Land of my Fathers
Gladiators: an amphitheatre of dreams
Beauty, brutality, in union
The hallowed turf: HQ
Sporting warfare: the ultimate prize
Victory, nationalistic pride
Bread of Heaven, Sweet Chariot
A stadium in chorus
Father, son: patriots hand in hand
Tension, expectation
Climax: winner, loser
Jubilation, aching despair
Admiration, humility
Regroup: until we go again

Barry Granger

THE VISIT

David Hockney, Mr and Mrs Clark and Percy, *1971*

It's seven o'clock of a June evening;
I call on them to talk it over.

The white telephone, which they keep on the floor,
catches light filtered through half-open shutters.

Walls seem to exude mushroom, layering beige
onto the carpet, into the air we breathe.

He's slouched in the metal chair; she, standing tall,
has hands on hips. Outside pigeons are cooing,

sounding loud in this poised room.
I decide to speak: Have you found anywhere yet?

A yellow directory lies unopened on a pale blue table.
Their silence is mutinous.

I explain again my need: the deadline.
Even the white cat sits rigid, his back to me,

attention focused on the leylandii outside.
I leave with the scent of lilies tight in my throat.

Sue Chadd

HIS FATHER

he's afraid he's like his father

I say *if you're worried about it*
you're not

he cuts his hair short
because he can't rebel against absence

his uncle coming round the corner
wants to punch him

so does our neighbour
from over the road

he is like his father

he says he might
get in touch with his father

meet him for lunch
once in a while

for although he's a fuck-up as a father
he's the only one he has

and he misses
his father

not the man
I offer to take him to see

the father he misses
is the one he thought he had

Deborah Harvey

BEGINNING

She's in the little blue car with him,
the car which lost a wheel in Essex,
broke down in Kent and Calais,
and will break down again,
although she cannot know this,
in Genoa and Montepulciano,
but now they're on their way,
rattling and chugging to the Alps
whose unexplored white heights
rear up ahead of them like
the married life they've just begun.

They plunge into the gloom of the new tunnel
and emerge in Italy. She leaves the car,
asks haltingly *Dove il gabinetto?*
then disappears down white stairs
freshly hollowed in the mountainside,
along passages, down more stairs,
seeing and hearing no-one.
Deep underground she slams
the cubicle's new-painted door,
then sees, too late, it lacks a handle.
Her calls of *Hello? Can someone help me?*
echo faintly and fade to silence.
Nothing to lose, she fills her lungs,
unleashes a fruity top-A yell
Aiuto! Aiuto! Nothing.
She remembers Verdi's entombed lovers
whose voices soar to welcome death.

Above ground he wonders
if marriage will mean love, curiosity,
concern sharpening into irritation.
He leaves the car, finds an official,
tastes the unfamiliar words
My wife... la mia moglie.
They descend and release her
from the porcelain underworld.
The little blue car lurches into their future
to the sound of raucous Italian laughter.

Pameli Benham

THE EVENSONG

I will not be long away
I told him at the gate
but it pleased me too much,
the road, the afternoon,
my strong new bicycle.

My lover warmed me more
than my husband's hearth.
It pleased me too much
to let the bell toll on
the road too long
the day too short
to go back home.

Husband and lover
were my world.
Now they are gone
but the same bell tolls
the evensong each day
and when I kneel to pray
for their two souls
it pleases me
how light still reaches in
from the west
to warm the stone.

I am growing old.
To my lover
I say in my prayers,
wait, I will not be long,
and to the other,
my husband, I whisper,
I will come home soon.
I have been too long gone.

Sue Boyle

FISH AUCTION

The old couple on the quay sort fish
with hands hard as hide from the tannery
down the lower end of town.
Eyes practised and steady scour this haul,
the scale-glinted curves that flip and slither to be weighed.

Men walk the box-sides inspecting,
exquisitely balance between quicksand catches,
ford the fish on stepping-stone crates.
The auctioneer gabbles prices
incomprehensible but to the cognoscenti
who flick responses like shook droplets.

A late fish shudders and arches,
springs off its pile of equals
and flops onto the quay.
No-one looks.
The fish-eye swivels, ceases, glazes.
Its body weight is bruised on stone.
It has nothing more to do with its element.

Beyond, the old couple take a breather,
the pause earned to wipe hands on coarse aprons
and exchange commentaries;
she laughs; he chews on plug.
The wide grey opening of ocean
flickers in rheumy eyes.

Zanna Beswick

READING MANDELSTAM

With a handful of images,
bronze coin,
he strung his song:

black earth   black sun
cathedral   apples   salt
          wine   snow

– how to take their measure,
strike one coin
against another?

Half a pulse later,
an echo of iron hoof-beats
drawing near.

Caroline Heaton

6

Solo Voices
Rosalie Challis

The working title for this section, I, Alone, was quickly changed after first study of its 15 poems. Far from being a collection of ego trips or of varied laments on isolation, what we have are strong, distinctive solo voices covering a range of themes common to poetry across the ages: childhood, love, loss, death, memory, dreams, imagination, creativity. As a group, the poems fall readily into a sequence tracing the familiar arc of the human condition, from our earliest days to the inevitability of death.

Morag Kiziewicz starts us on that journey with her lyrical first memories in This Is What I Remember. Its gently rocking repetition and beautiful details of the natural world capture memorably the delight of a very young child discovering 'the taste of spring'. For Ewan MacPherson early schooldays brought his first knowledge of acute sorrow and pain, with the consoling awareness in later years that this is sometimes how wisdom can be gained.

The next group of poems takes us beyond childhood years to three widely different experiences. Stewart Carswell not only stresses the life-saving aspect of singing but its tightly focused details evoke the unmistakable strains of a Welsh male voice choir. For Sara-Jane Arbury it is carpentry in its practical 'dove and tail' aspects which dominates in Wooden Dreams. Written 'after Lorraine Mariner', this poem shares fellow poet Mariner's liking for the everyday made quirky, even slightly surreal, combined with nicely placed flashes of wit. David Cohen also turns to humour in a wry, self-mocking poem in which his Tea Cup loses its lady owner's favours to a mug.

Moving through adult years brings more painful experiences of loss. In Tidying Drawers, Rachael Clyne's restrained description of a mundane task and small domestic problems heightens our sympathy as she deals with 'the crack in the fabric / of her world'. In Absence, Cathy Wilson turns round the loss her title implies by giving to this abstract noun the capacity to affect human senses with weight 'like a velvet cloak'.

The melancholy of the opening lines of Leanda Senior's poem What I Will Not Have is effectively countered by the conjuring of strikingly specific personal details. These take us to railway workers in Japan who, in the evocative final line, join the poet in sharing loss as part of our common humanity. Zanna Beswick's poem Always has England with the familiar sights and sounds of a shared home as its background. These set off memories for the poet which help compensate for the empty chair and provide reassurance that she will always be aware of 'the palpable skein of what love is'.

The first of Jay Arr's two impressive narrative poems, Paranoia, reveals what the narrator sees as the malign intent of mirrors to trick and deceive him. The tone is light, the language conversational but the result is an engrossing, often amusing monologue which, with clever irony, also gives a clear picture of the symptoms of persecution mania. His second poem, Special FX, is a subtle account of an encounter between himself as an adult and himself as a boy. Cathy Wilson's second poem centres on the names of boats moored in a harbour. One boat name, Night Hawk, captivates her and helps her create the fantasy of sailing out to adventure on the open sea. For Susan Utting in High Wire Act, imagination brings her to the challenging world of the tightrope walker. Set against the practical details of 'each well-chalked heel' is the alarming tension added by the chorus of rooks whose ability to fly gives the walker 'an urge to grow beyond the outstretch of my / finger ends'. The consequences of failure are chillingly evoked in this double-edged, 14-line drama.

The last two poems in Solo Voices focus on death, each in a highly original way. Cathy Wilson's Memento Mori follows the outline of Part IV of Tennyson's poem The Lady of Shalott. However, the narration has been changed, to memorable effect, from third person to the voice of the Lady. She claims the role of artist with one concern before sailing to certain death – that the world should know 'I wrote my name / before I pushed away'.

Finally comes Heidi Beck's Instructions for my Heirs. In the fine tradition of Dylan Thomas's defiant Do Not Go Gentle into That Good Night, she brings energy, courage and vision to the theme of death. Her leaps of imagination are astonishing, surging up like a great oratorio to peak in the fifth stanza, then slowing to the measured last couplet with its deeply moving repetition of the poem's first line. A wonderful close to the section, conveying vividly poetry's power to last beyond death, firing the imagination of successive generations of readers.

THIS IS WHAT I REMEMBER

These trees.
Their warmth and holding comfort
the bark throbbing with life, continuity
the gentle hill, my little legs toddling
past each tree, counting, not counting
the rhythm of shade.

This is what I remember. This river.
The rushing plunging torrent, the
sound a constant comfort, a bubbling
rippling rumbling flow. The roar of the river,
the churning of stones.

This is what I remember. Your garden.
Your planting and pruning, my hands digging finding
worms, snails, rich earth. Noticing snowdrops,
bluebells, brambles. Sweet berries,
the shape of leaves.

This is what I remember. Climbing
straw bales sun shifting jumping
in a golden storm.
The sound of rain thrumming.

This is what I remember. Wild roses.
The sound of celandines uncurling
lying on turf listening to birdsong
children, discovering the taste of spring.

Morag Kiziewicz

A PREP SCHOOL ME

A prep school me, somewhere in Kensington
Went walking in the rain to find some trees.
Then, there they were, sun-dappled in the square;
All quite locked up, so I could not come near.
I stood there wide-eyed, trying not to cry.
Above my tousled head the summer sky,
With cloudy shapes which slowly floated by.
I'd known no deeper sorrow in my life
Until my years were done and I would die.
The wisdom that we learn from pain like this
And then, sometimes, a strange and glowing joy
Cannot be found in books or manuscripts.
God writes them in the heart of every boy.
We do a pas de deux in time; beyond;
Between this ticking now and all to come.
It is as if, in moments such as these,
We flee the madness and we take our ease.
We walk on water when we face the sun;
And we and our inheritance are one.

Ewan A MacPherson

THROUGH SINGING

It is through singing that we breathe songs
so it is no wonder that here I am caged
by a singer with a voice like a coal seam
who sings not only as though his life depends on it,
but because ours do too.

Stewart Carswell

WOODEN DREAMS

after Lorraine Mariner

Some nights I dream about carpentry. Not the construction
of houses or flats, but more the dove and tail of it. The first cut
into a strip of timber, the knots, the lines, the fitting together.

In one dream I built the ark, upright and shipshape,
with a place for everything, including the woodworm.
When it floated across the world, I felt like God.

I did once have a carpentry pipe-dream: the one where I created
a tower out of planks, stretching right up to the heavens.
Its branches gathered the moon. Stars perched on its beams.

On nights I don't dream about carpentry,
I dream about woodcutting.
I wake with a splitting headache.

Sara-Jane Arbury

TEA CUP

Days of tedious waiting have
given way to months.
I used to be the frequent friend,
the cuppa worthy of his name.
Now supplanted by that mug.
Oh so well named in his
lumpen, fist-clenching awkwardness.
How I hate him for his favoured place.
Tea, coffee, cocoa, even sometimes
the frothing fizz of foaming pop.

Meanwhile I sit in dated elegance
at the back of my shelf, grateful
not to be strung up on a hook.

Not for me the daily kiss of
her ladyship's tender pink lips.
Not for me the exotic aroma
of Darjeeling, Lapsang Souchong
or even good old builders' tea.

Oh what I would give
for the shocking scalding liquid,
the onrush of colour and
the balming calm of a
dash of milk.

David Cohen

TIDYING DRAWERS

At last finding space to tidy
she adjusts the drawers
to sit flush with the chest
at the same time her life –
the semblance of control.

        Closing the crack in the fabric
        of her world, the departure
        so sudden; its aftershocks
        of a lost purse, power cuts,
        now subsiding.

It is comforting to know
how a drawer is held
together by dovetails
that it slides so easily back
into the cavern of a chest.

Rachael Clyne

ABSENCE

It lingers like fog after summer.
Unwanted at first
you grow accustomed to its weight
like a velvet cloak.

A trick of memory
it can conjure itself
from other sounds, the echoes
of feet, voices from the street.

A ghost, it shimmers
at the retina's edge
elusive as a mirage
real as a phantom limb.

Long after, it can still hit
sideways, like the odours
from a long unopened cupboard:
camphor, turpentine, seaweed.

Cathy Wilson

WHAT I WILL NOT HAVE

is someone to say 'Do you remember
how she could get lost on a postage stamp?'

Or that she sometimes kissed the underside of roses
for their cold silk smoothness on her mouth;

or that green was her favourite colour –
an exact shade of olive, worn by railway workers

in Japan. I can see them now, whistling a train
out of the station, one arm outstretched

and the track curving far off beyond my sight, and theirs.

Leanda Senior

ALWAYS

Sometimes the night brings him in
in the fold of a fox's bark
or the eager wailing of cats.
And you are sitting by the fireside
where the coals pursue their private Etna,
country of molten caverns,
the lava dragons shifting in their lair.
The pages of your book lie open,
the thronged words running on without you –
lives to be lived and fought out by chapter –
independent of attention.

You have your own stories dreaming themselves
in the rich tresses of memory,
all the tones of hope, anxiety, laughter, discontents,
the palpable skein of what love is.
You turn to meet its glance.

And night has brought him in.
The chair is empty,
the quiet hearth settled.
Yet just beyond sight
he stands in the silence where touch was,
enfolds you in the wings of rest.
Later will come the sharp tang of dawn;
stars fall to brighten grass,
the chattering pigeons, the early-rising pheasant.
Still lingers the embrace,
unspoken now, transcendent.

Zanna Beswick

PARANOIA

My concern is mirrors,
their insistence on correction
for making left, right.

I've tried: sneaking
up on them from behind
– no good;

waiting till dark,
surprising them with a torch,
they were ready.

I suspect, when they're alone
they practise to perfect inversion.
I've seen them together

paralleled, multiplying
like rabbits, and other
perversions.

Try bending them to your will
and they'll distort reality,
make things closer the farther

they are behind. And don't be fooled
by their benign reflection,
apparently seeing only what

you want to see.
Imagine what they collect,
reflect, when you are not there.

And their dark magic,
they are masters of the slow, subtle change.
In them did you, did things, look the same

and High Wire a day, a week, a year ago? No.
Notice, when you're not looking,
the sly winks they exchange

that say one day,
one day, we will stand
the world on its head.

Jay Arr

SPECIAL FX

Night backstreeting I followed the wynd,
maze-muddled at every corners' blind

turn. Lost. Confused. I tried the trick
of finger-feel way-marking the change of brick

but in that evening's last glim of summer light
the strung-out ghosts of washing hazed my sight

of the miniature meteor tracking out of the gloom;
it was zeroed-in, locked on to the curtained room,

had targeted the window pane. From over the wall
I'd heard the whack, the claimant's call

for six, the counter yell of four, before
my instinctive hand stop relished the brief sore

of success; when, from out of the dark ran
my young self to a stop. Same boy. Same man.

Had one stepped forward or the other back
to make the strike, the lucky catch, into that lack

of light? *Here*, said self to self handing over the ball.
Thanks, he replied, returning to the game. That was all

we exchanged across the years. I still wonder, did I know
it was me or had time's film flipped deliberately to show

that, whatever the play in the fade flickered light,
the pane never shatters, the spool always loops back

and back into the night.

Jay Arr

NIGHT HAWK

Walking round the harbour
eyeing the boats
I overhear a father
playing pretend with his son –
Which one is yours, then?

He could have read my thoughts.

And I would answer: all and none.
Not Melinda
or Jason.
Not Aleta, or Dawn.

I might offer a cautious nod
to Skara Brae
to Windhover
to Wanderer.

Never Flash, or Surprise.

Only at night, is it mine
this fragile scintilla
in its scoop of winking
harbour.

For I am Night Hawk –
I slip past anchor lines
skirting Obsession
and Mistral, out to sea.

Cathy Wilson

HIGH WIRE ACT

Up here the rooks are noisy, welcome me
with open wings, they recognise the look
in my eye: beady, steely some might say,
but steady, always steady, like the single file
of heel to toe, heel to toe, the easy glide across.

But there are days I feel a pricking at my back,
the scapulas' itch, a budding under my skin,
an urge to grow beyond the outstretch of my
finger ends. And I have felt my insteps lift,
each well-chalked heel give up the wire,

give in to risk, the stretch and push to tiptoe.
Then I have heard the ruffling of plumage, caw
and screech, have seen the zigzag down through
air that will not hold a feather's weight, its fall.

Susan Utting

MEMENTO MORI

inspired by Alfred Tennyson's
The Lady of Shalott

How black the river looms, how still
its world of upside down
the willow branches swaying
as if they
might break my fall.

And how the boat
glides on now, urgent as a swan.

Rush lights gutter at my side –
how clear their whispers sound
like the chatter below
the towered room
where I wove and sang.

Let no-one say I spent my days
half-sick of shadows.

I made my own way
to this shore,
the cradle
that waited.

Let them say: I laid my head
against its sleek, dark neck.
That I wrote my name
before I pushed away.

Cathy Wilson

INSTRUCTIONS FOR MY HEIRS

Do not put me in a box.
No gathered satin pinned with nails, no lid.
Let the coffin-maker starve.

I do not fear an endless night
laid out beneath retreating stars,
but not for me the claggy freight of soil.

Put me on a mountaintop, exposed
so wind can flay and shear my flesh.
Let microbes clear my bones until they clatter.

Or put me on a pyre, let me burn,
my vapours stretching for the stratosphere.
Let me be the dust that seeds the rain.

Find me in the air, the space,
the gaps between the pixels on this page.
I will be the oscillation,

the compression and release of waves.
Launch me. Let me sail.
Do not put me in a box.

Heidi Beck

7

A Fine Line
Claire Dyer

Ekphrasis is a rhetorical device in which one medium of art tries to relate to another by describing its essence and form, and what is fascinating is how the poets whose work is to follow have taken up this challenge. Elsewhere in this anthology, the edge of the sea is described as a 'liminal world that is neither land nor water', and the poems in this section demand and give much on both sides of an equally ambiguous world.

The poems concentrate not so much on landscapes and backgrounds but on the people who inhabit them. Whether these people be fictional or real or the poets themselves, it is they who attract the eye and engage the heart.

To me, the poems in this section of the book suggest a triptych, with those in the first panel representing specific works of art. In Reflections on 'Family Fishing', the poet translates a moment in time, she tells us of stasis and the ultimate disconnectedness of people, whereas in Resurrection we learn about rapture and connectedness, 'the love that is always being made'. This spilling of emotion is explored further in The Arnolfini Marriage, the bride speaking to us directly from the 15th century and asking us hard questions about how we see and judge her. In Annetje Remembers, a mother recalls her lost daughter when polishing a funeral spoon; yet again, it is the intangible which is conjured from the tangible, how 'The curve of her smile' can be invoked from something seen, something held. Conversely, the artist in Self Portrait is asking his poet, as she looks at him, to reveal something of herself; another kind of relationship entirely. The three responses to The Man in a Hat conclude this panel for me: we are spoken to directly by him, we hear from a former lover, and we engage in a dialogue in which we are given no voice. In all instances, as with the poet's narrators, we have to understand our own unreliability and learn to trust in the illusory: 'at night I shall / watch the Dog Star in the dark fields race / after the shrieking hare'.

The second panel of my triptych concerns itself with the experience of being painted. In Likeness there is an unspoken contract between artist and sitter to produce, '*A lovechild, some say. / Not yours. Not mine.*' In Being Painted, Ray Fussell wryly acknowledges the relationship between vanity and identity, a theme extended in The Artist as His Studio, where it seems that the poet's and artist's sense of mutual dependence is a wonderful hybrid of discomfort and admiration. Rosie Jackson's specular poem makes much of this bond between the one who draws and the one being drawn, a childhood meeting with an artist proving one which would lead the poet to vow to 'be her, / able to magic away absence'. It is, however, a different kind of absence which is explored in The Sitters. Here the absence of reality, the gap between how we really see ourselves and what lies beneath is painfully portrayed. By responding to the previous poem in its acknowledgement of the ache in this gap between reality and art – 'You will create me / So that even I don't recognise myself' – Sitting for a Portrait segues into the final panel of my imaginary triptych.

Marilyn Monroe, Cleopatra and Helen of Troy figure in two of the poems in this final panel, which I see as the necessary evolution of the previous two. In Warhol Blonde, the poet is asking us to see the photographic negative, not the actual – to see beyond, behind and beneath the colours of the 50 images of Warhol's Marilyn to what we may have forgotten about who Marilyn really was. As if to show us the solid truth of this, in The Art of Portraiture we are told what it is within the artist's power to do, how 'Each brush stroke bears / a fragment of soul rough with tears'. However, with power comes responsibility and so in Portrait of a Young Woman the representation of an anonymous woman wearing a jade earring becomes all women, from Eve onwards. The penultimate poem, Group Critique at Dove Street is about a communal response to art framed within the very personal, 'the colour of a room; / a film clip of this street, with my hands / in close-up'.

I have begun and ended this section with the poems A Fine Line and Capturing the Light. The opening poem describes the specific light a poem can shed, 'like a spotlight on the performer / who illuminates only what is necessary'. The final poem gifts us an appreciation of the words we can use in our attempt to define light, and shapes the meanings they can give us. However, as with most forms of art, our vision and our understanding is drawn away from the immediate to where our imaginations can take flight, as though by looking at Vermeer's girl we see not her, not a colour, but 'the light of buttercups, / as if to her face she had raised / an acre, a field, of them'.

A FINE LINE

This poem has to be concise like a portrait:
too many brush strokes
and the image becomes blurred,
too few and it is underdeveloped.
A fine line exists where the identity
and intention are revealed,
a balance between weight and flight
like a spotlight on the performer
who illuminates only what is necessary.

Stewart Carswell

REFLECTIONS ON 'FAMILY FISHING'

after Henri Rousseau, View of the Quai d'Ivry
near the Port à l'Anglais, Seine, *1900*

This is how Sundays might appear
for a tidy man, a toll collector say,
living a safe life, spending time
with his family
by a lake in a small town.

Except for these three –
man, woman and unwatched baby –
the scene is unpeopled.
A flat-bottomed boat wallows
on the slab of empty water.

The woman is silent
as she watches her husband
dribble his feeble line,
knows he will catch nothing.
Knows too, that if he wasn't fishing
he would be painting –
each layer of oiled colour applied
in patient strokes, smooth and formal
as the clipped lawns and relentless path
chaperoning the lake side.

Hard to see what brings them out here
together, yet apart, their faces
like pressed flowers, turned
forever sideways.

Behind their backs, rubbing
shoulders with the signature,
a huddle of shapes
like pigeons.

Perhaps Rousseau
meant them to be shrubs.
I so want them to be birds –
rapid-sketched
greedy, noisy, nerve-sprung
a wing-clap from flitting
this sticky corner of half-lived days.

Cathy Wilson

RESURRECTION

after Stanley Spencer, The Reunion

And suddenly they are streaming back from the dead,
unburying themselves,
their tombstones mere props for gossip
now the final day has come.

Only this is not the last day,
but the first of an eternal summer
where loss turns back into desire,
for what can match the pleasure of a kiss
on the tongue of those grown accustomed to tasting nothing?

Nothing more glorious for those whose senses were lost
than these arms around the loved one's shoulder,
the conjugal embrace, the breasts
that never bruise with too much touching,
the heavy angels spilling out of windows and doors
to welcome them home.

This is what they dreamt of ascending to:
gardens, allotments, lamps pooling light over dinner.
This what they longed to recapture:
reaching round a chest that rises and falls,
the rapture of breath that doesn't stop.

Flesh ripe with joy now they are touching again,
lovers, mothers, children, fathers, plumped-up wives,
in this light that is never switched off,
these bodies that cannot have enough of each other,
this love that is always being made.

Rosie Jackson

THE ARNOLFINI MARRIAGE

after Jan Van Eyck

What's to make of it – me, in my voluptuous dress,
my palm as clear as innocence, as smooth as oil
on canvas, touching his. And there are oranges,
exotic signals of fecundity, an apple, still un-bitten
and that single candle lit above his head. Above my
cast off slippers, un-ringed fingers, dream-cast eyes,
there are the red and velvet draperies, the richness
of that covered, canopied in crimson bed.

There is no mystery – we're pictured back to innocence,
composed in symmetry, respectable and un-dishevelled;
truth is we were just too full of loving, much too full
of having loved each other, there, just then, and often,
to have thought what centuries would make of it.

Susan Utting

ANNETJE REMEMBERS

Funeral Spoon, Amsterdam, 1665

She takes a piece of worn cloth, passes
her fingers round the spoon's smooth edge,
trying to soothe her year-long grief.

She recalls her newborn's curled fist
in the hollow of her palm, feels once more
the pang of bonding with her only daughter.

In the spoon's fine stem she sees again
her girl's slender limbs, when she lifted her
from the tub, dried her beside the fire.

Lisabet, willow slim, moving through kitchen
and yard, washing beakers and platters,
spreading wet clothes out to dry.

The curve of her smile, her eyes,
grey like the North Sea, more
precious than a king's ransom in silver.

Rosalie Challis

SELF PORTRAIT

after Diego Velázquez

Señor, you seem to offer me
your head upon a platter, poised
on the tilted ruff of a Spanish courtier.

Four centuries close to an arm's length
as we take each other in. Younger than me
behind that lustrous hair and tipped moustache
yet a cushion of flesh under the chin, shadows
around the eyes reveal the artist
knew his sitter well.

My gaze, fulfilled and restless, turns
away, but your eyes invite me
to be their focus of desire,
where my deep regard raises you
from the dead, as yours recalls me
to all I have been avoiding:
Quítese esos velos, ya, Señora!
Lady, remove your veils…

Jill Sharp

THE MAN IN A HAT

i. Aftermath

When all this is over, said the man
in the black fedora, I will pack a small case
and fly to a country

where no-one has heard of me
and my fingerprints appear on no database.
My name will be my mother's,

silk cut in the mouth, at night I shall
watch the Dog Star in the dark fields race
after the shrieking hare.

ii. A former lover recalls...

'Ah, your eyes like pale fire,
the sable fur stroking
your throat! how could I

have known my fingers
would learn to covet
the soft wizened flesh

of your quisling's neck
so much more than your
gifted, exquisite mouth?'

iii. Interview

[Throat clearing]
You see, it was needful. We had no choice.
Nor, before you ask, any regrets, these things

happen in war. Oh yes, for those present,
unlike your good self, it was war. Our own

mothers, even, turned out to be as culpable
as the rest. So it had to be dealt with at night,

otherwise things would have got out of hand,
barricades, brick-throwing, looting: imagine it –

another twenty-four hours of sitting idle
and it would have spread to the suburbs,

then east to the camps, all over. What we did
was inevitable; clean sweep, fresh start. *[Pause]*

No more questions. *[End]*

Lesley Saunders

LIKENESS

Please sit. Sit how you like.
And talk. Talk if you like.
Until mouth. When mouth, lips closed.
Shadows of buddleia blow on the window.

Pinned to the wall, a row of your creatures,
hybrids in paint and sable, tone and shade.
Gold leaf reverences them.
What undisclosed sadness
did you conjure in powdered pigment?

Please move. Move if you like.
But not now. Now mouth.
I'm drawing your mouth.
The paper is clipped to your easel.

The portrait
like breath on water.
A lovechild, some say.
Not yours. Not mine.

Nikki Kenna

BEING PAINTED

Curiosity invites.
Vanity takes a shower, washes hair,
brushes teeth, and picks a shirt.
Routine drives to the bus, travels to town,
has a panini in Nero's with coffee.
Patience does some shopping to kill time.
Resilience walks through the rain to the studio.
Ego shows interest in the artist's work.
Discipline sits still.
Self-consciousness fills the air with chatter.
Vanity returns to look at the portrait.

Ray Fussell

THE ARTIST AS HIS STUDIO

for Malcolm Ashman

Maps lie. The studio's half an inch at most from the car park.
I call him after ten minutes' walk. You're halfway here, he says.
After another half mile, he comes out, waits with a smile
and a maze of passageways.

By the door, signage announces this is a shrine.
I pause. Wonder, should I take off my shoes. Decide not.
At head height am greeted by a dead, pink, jellyfish;
which is not.

Rather a bedraggled fire balloon once rescued, and notice
on the far wall shades of purple, puce and dirty yellow escape
from a printer's font-tray above a lagged stopcock.
Walls are white.

Carrier bags – ex-Vivienne Westwood, Selfridges and Pink – hang from
            nails.
There's nothing in them. On the floor, shoes pair, line up and point.
Suspended from a rail, a lonely wicker basket keeps vigil.
Empty.

An orange disconsolate hairdryer, a frame of honeycomb keep company
                                    with…
What's this? I ask. *My shrine; people give me things*, he says, pointedly.
I rummage through pockets
and don't.

Walls are still. And white. A saw yellow with a red handle, climbs a wall
by
                              the door
whose back says, 'Keep Calm and Carry On'. His paintings have taken
      refuge
                                    on a shelf.

A princely face with crown doubles as a mug, scissors and pencils poke
into
                              hair.
Almost real.

Here's lamp black nuzzling up to Scheveningen's warm greys,
while Old Holland lies with Winsor & Newton's iridescent
white.
A citron yellow, boxed with verdigris green.
Sorted.

He's uneasy with his easel, which is wobbly;
Stop talking, I'm doing your mouth,
and I do
and he does.

At last, I'm allowed to look.
It looks like me, I say
and hear him think,
They all say that.

Jay Arr

COULD YOU MAKE MY MOUTH SMILE MORE?

Sitting to have my portrait drawn,
everything goes back to that night when I was four:
sneaking downstairs through the dark, meeting a stranger
in the lamplight, where I'd expected to find my mother.
Lying in this young woman's lap, drawings of bodies:
baby, gorgeous from all angles,
hands, arms, legs, a nude – my first.
And what a wondrous likeness of me: my tousled curls,
my sleeping child's mouth half-open, hungry for the world.
This was the woman I wanted to be: unafraid of nakedness.
How did I get to be a magician who conjured up a person
out of nothing? Who made this child? What was this secret
of lines and shapes, this mystery of creating life?
If I could do what she had done, lost in a trance
of deft flesh on white space, I would no longer be alone,
never again without this company –
shoulders, eyebrows, ankles, knees, kisses –
a mother joined to her baby in one line.
That night I fell in love, vowed I would be her,
able to magic away absence. Remembering,
I ask the artist to make my mouth smile a little more –
sitting for my new portrait,
legs crossed, shoulders slightly hunched,
a perfect rose on my jacket.

A perfect rose on my jacket,
legs crossed, shoulders slightly hunched,
sitting now for my new portrait,
I ask the artist to make my mouth smile a little more,
able to magic away absence. Remembering
that night I fell in love, vowed I would be her:
a mother joined to her baby in one line –
shoulders, eyebrows, ankles, knees, kisses –
never again without this company
of deft flesh on white space. I would no longer be alone,
if I could do what she had done, lost in a trance
of lines and shapes, this mystery of creating life
out of nothing. Who made this child? What was this secret?
How did I get to be a magician who conjured up a person?
This was the woman I wanted to be, unafraid of nakedness,
my sleeping child's mouth half-open, hungry for the world.
And what a wondrous likeness of me: my tousled curls,
hands, arms, legs, a nude – my first
baby gorgeous from all angles,
lying in this young woman's lap. Drawings of bodies
in the lamplight, where I'd expected to find my mother
sneaking downstairs through the dark, meeting a stranger.
Everything goes back to that night when I was four,
sitting to have my portrait drawn.

Rosie Jackson

THE SITTERS

1
We who come to sit,
what do we hope to discover
in this small whitewashed cell
with its two plain wooden chairs?

When curiosity finds us
helpless as a bunch of grapes
under the steely eyes of the artist,
what kind of reward for this do we expect?

The challenge is not to resist
whatever truth lives in shape or colour.
To meet the artist's gaze. Then the gaze
of that familiar unfamiliar person in the frame.

2
And yet –
when we said, *Tell it like it is,*
we were not meaning this:

Not meaning the pen and ink lines
that appear to be stubble on that (female) chin.
Not meaning a white face naive as a new-baked loaf,
something blatantly coquettish
about the way we turn our heads to look at you
looking at us. Not meaning a nugget of stone
apparent in the throat or the unblinking
luminous gaze of someone crazy
for the cold blade of a knife. Not meaning
the straight line of a crenellated, thin top lip,
the shoulders that never shrug. Not meaning
everything in monotone. Not meaning the wince
creased into the forehead as you find us out,
the hair twisted, the brow pleated
through thinking too much, eyes behind glass
seeing more than they want. Not meaning

more loveliness than we have ever possessed.
Not meaning, for a single breath, our hearts
hung at our throats. Not meaning the mask
stripped away to expose the vulnerable bones.

When we offered to sit for you,
this was not what we were meaning.
This was not what we meant.

Postcript

And to sit
in the confusion of the twenty-first century,
simply taking one breath after another,
this too is an art.

Chrissy Banks

SITTING FOR A PORTRAIT

I can give you Marilyn Monroe lips if you like,
and yes, I believe you can,
better than God,
better than my parents ever could.

I am an original, here to be reborn
from the tip of your pencil.
Please, erase the mistakes,
no surgeon ever managed to do that.

The canvas stands pale as a bed sheet.
Leave your mark and make me
in your image, let private sight
notice the fingers on my hands,

the particular way my face falls.
Noses are difficult, and I'm there
when Eve came, fashioned from bone
with the most perfect nose.

You will create me
so that even I don't recognise myself –
Can you see you? Yes, I'm sure
that's my jawline, my posture,

the hint of a smile
thinning my lips, all temptation
for Marilyn's full-bodied pout rubbed out
in the copied blink of my eye.

Sara-Jane Arbury

WARHOL BLONDE

What you don't remember is the way
she fades to smudge, to mono-
chrome, to feint, to whiteout.

You don't forget the yellow hair,
the slash of a carmine mouth,
that charcoal edge, the turquoise

lids that match the wings
of a stand-up collar; or the clash
of tangerine behind the linctus

pink of skin. There she is,
twice five times five, all half-
closed eyes and kiss-me pout,

a set of flick-book movie stills,
again, again and over, nothing
changing but the colours.

What shocks you now is not
acrylic zing or canvas weave,
the irony of mock-naive repeat,

it's what you see you had
forgotten: all that shadow,
its hide and seek, its chill.

Susan Utting

THE ART OF PORTRAITURE

A face is more than flesh and bone
captured on camera, features that droop,
a nose no mirror will diminish. While Photoshop
can airbrush imperfection so that tone
trumps fidelity, it tricks us into adoration
of chimeras, loveliness turned carnival mask
smiling horror. Artists reach
past skin as if to prove the weight of being
sequestered inside tiny sparks of pigment.
Paint on canvas is a condign medium for
the mess of life lived; truth is not *de facto*
beautiful. Each brush stroke bears
a fragment of soul rough with tears,
like marks out of ten for effort.

Shirley Wright

PORTRAIT OF A YOUNG WOMAN

She is Nefertiti,
Cleopatra smouldering for Rome,
she is Isis and the Nile
is all her tears,
she is the girl with the jade earring,
a face that's launched
at least a thousand ships,
La Belle Dame Sans Merci,
hauteur and mystery of the divine
hung for us on bee-stung lips,
pouting, petulant, impossible.
She is the template, the crucible,
Adam's first dream.

Shirley Wright

GROUP CRITIQUE AT DOVE STREET

Brittle bird-bones of an idea are spread
across the floor, in a line of abstract reliefs,
pale blocks split by paint or shadow.
Gesturing, we step over drawings,
fingers tight round mugs of tea,
careful of what we might spill.

The studio window frames the city.
A blue girder bridge counterbalances
the silver lines of the shopping centre.
A small rectangle of ruby wall
is intersected by a gull's flight.

Cartridge paper lies skew over brushes.
On a pile of books, a portrait of a man.
Biscuits are opened, passed round.
We watch each other's faces, assess
the small precise changes between
what is said and what is not.

Being back in Bristol stirs me up.
The past is framed less precisely:
smudged portraits; the colour of a room;
a film clip of this street, with my hands
in close-up, a map open.

The city is a sea of mutable greys.
Dove Street curls past the Centre
for The Deaf. Memory unspools
thirty years to a spring day here,
and a silent crowd talking,
hands fluttering like birds.

Clare Diprose

CAPTURING THE LIGHT

Not that it can be captured – only held,
briefly,
as it passes at the speed of itself
through the retina, the lens, the *camera lucida*.

Think of the words we owe
to its visible difference:
luminescence, glow-worm, illumination, halo,
crepuscular, blind.

We can play tricks with it,
and do – look at Vermeer's
Officer and Laughing Girl, for instance:
before taking in the shadowed view

of the hat, the glass, the map, all we see
is the girl, gleamy with the light of buttercups,
as if to her face she had raised
an acre, a field, of them.

Leanda Senior

8

Landscapes of the Mind
Sue Boyle

Many of the poems in this section take us on journeys of exploration and discovery, journeys away from the familiar and journeys of return. The destinations are real. They have their own resonant, often intriguing names – Drogheda, Quoyness, Carnac, Wild Boar Fell – and come alive in these poems because their poets know them viscerally and convey this knowledge with such sensitivity and skill. This is writing of intimate engagement. The poems give us opportunities to travel into the core of our relationship with elemental places, places often so uncluttered by the paraphernalia of our urban industrial existence that we can feel for the moment that we have stepped out of history and out of time. They give us landscapes of water, air and stone through which human figures move in silence, or near silence, alert to every nuance of light, weather, sound. Much of the writing is as uncluttered as the landscapes and sparse in its language and imagery, which gives it an especially powerful imaginative charge:

> *The droplet of an iceberg melting.*
> *The mirror moisture of a dying man.*

The journeys in these poems are not metaphors, but many of them use the powerfully suggestive duality of metaphor to offer us parallel journeys into the essence of being human, journeys of life and death, light and dark, journeys into meaning and mystery. The opening poem, Drogheda by Sara Butler, establishes this theme with its image of the sun finding its way to 'the heart of things'. The idea of one place being at the same time the place of arrival at the heart of darkness and the 'final opening into a view' is echoed in Linda Saunders' intriguing The Maze towards the section's end. Both these poems have the vividness and open-endedness of myth, somethingwhich underwrites many of the pieces here. A strong sense of myth and prehistory also links Ama Bolton's Chambered Cairn, Ewan MacPherson's Mendip and Caroline Heaton's Other Megaliths. That long poem, like Susan Jane Sims' much shorter Return Journey, enacts the necessary equilibrium and tension between the surface of our everyday familiar world and the deep spaces that a good poem can help us to explore. Children play hide and seek at the mouth of the dolmen; the 'old skin' shed for the duration of the poem's journey waits patiently to be resumed at the return. In Clare Diprose's wonderful image, 'A raven rises on the wind. We meet / Our own footprints coming up'.

Footprints, traces and echoes are all powerful ideas in this sequence of poems. The effort of attention which is required to follow footprints, to become attuned to the hints and echoes of vanished lives and distant histories is the perfect metaphor for the effort of attention required to travel to the core of poems like these and hear what they have to say. Most are saying much more than is apparent on their surfaces. We often grasp their stories less through statement than through the eloquence of suggestion and the discretion of their silences. Also through the power of their haunting visual images – souls rising 'tall in the moonlight', fog shaping itself like a flying swan, parched creatures 'picking their way gently over the cracked earth', the Howgills 'so still in their gravid dream'.

These are poems of epic journey, intensely focused with a fine specificity of detail and attention to the moment. You return from reading this section as if from a feast of new experience and new places, extended and enriched.

DROGHEDA

I know this place,
this passage tomb, these silent stones,
this corbelled roof and the sun
that finds its way to the heart of things.

Sara Butler

CHAMBERED CAIRN

Quoyness, 2008

The passage is three feet high:
on your knees in the seething dark you enter.
In the corbelled chamber's space
you uncoil and stand earth-fast at the centre.

The silence sings in your ears.
On an inch of paper you write the three runes
of your name, bind it with hair
and hide it in a crevice between the stones.

Ama Bolton

SMALL STEPS FOR MAN

The anxious breath of a newborn child.
The atom in a hydrogen bomb.

The song of spring's dawn chorus.
The bubble of an offshore oil leak.

The snowdrop breaking frozen soil.
The plastic shred in the Pacific.

The droplet of an iceberg melting.
The mirror moisture of a dying man.

Ray Fussell

MENDIP

In Mendip's limestone land, the caves are dark
And sheep are grazing where the Romans walked.
Below the hill where Priddy Church now stands,
The Mattins over and the people left,
I saw the travellers camping on the green
And heard their Irish voices with delight.
Up on the Batch, the path the old Celts knew
Was dusty grey and stone-lined fields beyond.
Wide spread the farmsteads in this ancient place;
No Saxon closeness in these hallowed hills.
In centuries they've never known a drought.
Dips in the land catch the primeval dew.
I walk in cassock down to the New Inn
And bless the day I found this lovely place.

Ewan A MacPherson

LACUNA

The land appears and evaporates
like short-term memory.

Across the Levels – silence.

The fog conjures itself briefly
into the weighty body and outstretched
neck of a single swan –

a regal barque sailing the air
of a floating world.

Rachael Clyne

WEIGHING SOULS

It being All Hallows
I set a hessian bag upon my door
for the Weighing of Souls.
Mother, father, brother,
my sister's unlucky child,
last, my own sweet half-way babe
laid in the earth unpriested,
all are welcome here
this clear-sky night.
The bag waits open-mouthed.

I close my eyes to see my souls rising
tall in the moonlight,
the babe slipping between them
as I sometimes see him
between his sisters at play.
But like a weak-willed disciple
I let sleep take me, and although cockcrow
finds the bag a little heavier
only the weight of November fog
seeps through its weave.

And I must carry my souls with me
cradled in my heart another twelvemonth.

Louise Green

TRACKS

A fox's neat snow-prints in a single line
cross the double dot and dash of a rabbit.

Each grass stem carries a wind-trace,
a thin slipstream of ice.

In the lee of the hill,
red sandstone outcrops in snowdrifts.

Low sun stretches each shadow,
heaves up ripples in the rock.

We rub the grit with gloved hands,
grasp its story through our summers:

the hiss of an incoming tide,
ridges of damp sand under bare feet.

Below us, a dark valley falls away
to the distant estuary

where children's footprints in the ooze
have turned to stone.

A raven rises on the wind. We meet
our own footprints coming up.

Clare Diprose

OTHER MEGALITHS

Loosed from our own moorings,
we jettison Carnac, settle for other megaliths,
watching for the tiny bobbing boat to stop at the quay.
It sinks a little beneath each step, buoys us
over green water to where the currents pitch
and alarm blooms on the children's faces.
Then the water blows smooth again, brings us to the bay –
Locqmariaquer, lapped with legends of drowned lords.

The café is a brief haven, where wooden tables
and benches soothe us with their solid surfaces,
before the bar-girl with a map of the megaliths
speeds us on, but twenty minutes from the café
there are fractured paving stones at the wrong-turn,
rusty earth we scuff into our sandals
and suddenly it's here again, disorientation,
like a sorry dog, tagging my footsteps –

and this piece of abroad is barely anchored
with invented purpose. I'm swinging
on a slack rope between home and home,
and the children droop like flowers out of rain
till they spot the sign to a vast field of stones
and run to play hide and seek
at death's entrance, the dolmen hole,
plait grass-blades in its shadow.

The field stretches shelterless, a huge menhir
lying broken on the ground beside the tumulus
with its bare corridor of stones.
Are these inhuman dimensions, this aridity
what we have come to see,
listening to a Chinese guide enumerate
stone heights and breadths, burying us
beneath their brute tonnage?

As she speaks, I dizzy with immensities
and swelter again in the furnace
of a Neolithic summer, wondering
at the remote faith which built
not these megaliths, but man's first straw villages,
a scratched security on the harsh plains,
families and livestock poised precariously
between red earth – red star.

Caroline Heaton

THE LISTENING WALK

Brag, sweet tenor bull,
descant on Rawthey's madrigal.
Basil Bunting, *Briggflatts*

We straggle apart across a stubble field,
tuned in to the rasp of straws, squeak-clunk
of a kissing-gate, our own breath as we climb
to the solitary oak, its bell of shade.

Not a shiver of wind or chitter of bird:
volume not of sound but of the tree's living
silence, holding the centuries still
under today's unblemished sky.

We question distance beyond the near scuff
of boots and cloth as we walk on, for some faint
man-made thrum, or hum along wires, or
a first rumour of the unseen Rawthey.

So acute has our hearing become, almost
we catch the Quakers' voices released
from the folds of years, and their silence ring
in the Meeting House behind the bull's sweet echo.

The quiet hangs in a haze that softens the fells
dozing at their watch on the edge of things.
And the size of it finds an inward
reflection, a land unsounded in our selves.

Only the river – yes, now! – in its hushed rush
below the steep wood's crook clucks
and mutters its garbled gossip, flashing
between the alders, quick tongues.

Linda Saunders

Basil Bunting named his poem for the Quaker meeting house,
Briggflatts, near the Howgill fells, close to the river Rawthey.

SCHERZO / ANDANTE

Stenniskeugh Clouds

Seen from the valley:
                   a raft of cloud
seems to hang below the shoulder
of Wild Boar Fell, whose high prow cuts
through an ice-flow of cirrus.

Underfoot, it's stone:
                best dance it,

dodging ruck and gryke, the next step
redeeming the last, and each an instant
decision with an eye to the lie of it,
to that pavement you'll stride on
a few easy yards into the wind.

Now a rest:
             and it ages to inveterate
stillness, a skin pocked and wizened
to ungloved fingers, under your scrutiny
of the lichens' patience.

Then the view:
             the Howgills, so still

in their gravid dream, though the wind
must be streaming their unfenced grass,
and a salvo of shadows could be
wild sooty horses making a dash,
as if on the wind's or a thought's impulse,
then a stop –
             no note as dark
and sudden to the heart
against the hill's bleached sail.

Linda Saunders

THE MAZE

for S J Litherland

Veteran of argument, how could she resist
pitting her own determination
against the maze? And I followed her,
between walls built into the hillside
like a ruined thumbprint.

I thought us pieces in a children's game,
intrepid spirits defiant of age,
till something between submission
and reverence surprised me
in her careful tread.

I noticed her head and shoulders bowed
under a mantilla of shadow,
and sensed the knot we walked in,
fate and our own wits entwined in a paradox
that tightened at every turn.

As we wound and climbed, the sand
beneath our bare feet turned to snow,
and that pain eclipsed all other challenge
as we trudged on – towards the centre
or final opening into a view.

Linda Saunders

FROM A DISTANCE

Watch from a distance:
see how the leathery ones come
picking their way gently
over the cracked earth.

Watch the matriarch: how even now
she shows her young followers
how to trace the contours
of bleached bone and bark.

Watch the circle thicken, widen,
drop to its knees as one
before a long forgotten sun god.
Watch, from a distance

as the blackness falls.

Susan Jane Sims

ORKNEY: KIRKWALL TO TANKERNESS

Leap for the verge! This road's
too busy for its two lanes.

Ponies graze next to the airport,
knee-deep in buttercups:

the mid-day flight to Aberdeen
worth merely a twitch of an ear.

Pause for a purple orchid.
Lean on a gate to sketch

a flock of fuchsias in the shelter
of a barn without a roof

the twist of a sycamore by the burn
and a tin house with broken windows.

Press on to Mine Howe
earth's open mouth

pay the entrance fee
climb down the dark stair

stand rooted in the past
feast on silence

heart jumping
in the kist of bones.

Ama Bolton

RETURN JOURNEY

Mull lets us slip anchor
as quietly as it welcomed us.
No fanfare, no hullabaloo.
We travellers who called
the island home
for a few short days
now slip from view
as the ferry drinks the miles.

There's something sad
about a journey in reverse
the slow unwind
from the place we've reached
and the person we've become,
shrugging on our old skin,
slotting back into the life
that's been waiting patiently
for our return.

Susan Jane Sims

The poets

SARA-JANE ARBURY lives in Bristol. She has been involved in the production and promotion of creative writing and live literature for 20 years, collaborating with organisations including the Arts Council, the BBC, Oxford University Press and Bloodaxe Books. Sara-Jane was the Voices Off Director at Cheltenham Literature Festival, the first Writer-in-Residence for Herefordshire and is the co-founder of Spiel Unlimited with fellow writer and raconteur Marcus Moore.
Pamphlets: *Gutted* (PotA Press), *County Lines, Park Street Shuffle, Sweetie, The Day the Torch Came to Cheltenham* (Cheltenham Borough Council)
Anthologies: *Rive Gauche: Women Poets Writing and Performing in Bristol in the 1990s* (Rive Gauche Publishing), *The Bristol Slam Poetry Anthology* (PotA Press), *PROOF* (South West Arts), *The Village Shop Quartet* (Oxford Playhouse), *Velocity: The Best of Apples & Snakes* (Black Spring Press), *Bugged... Writings from Overhearings* (Bell Jar)

JAY ARR lives in Broadtown, Wiltshire, where he publishes an online ekphrastic poetry and art e-zine called *the IMPpress*, and has been the organiser and MC of the poetry café at the Marlborough Literature Festival for the past three years. He is a founder member of Swindon's BlueGate Poets. Now retired, after 40 years in the computer and communications industries working in the UK, Europe, Scandinavia, the USA and Japan, he designs and builds websites for friends, publishes poetry pamphlets and gives occasional poetry workshops and readings.
Book: *A Machine for Measuring Blue*
Pamphlets: *and what did you want?, nietsa, poems from the private life of gargoyles, she is new as a city*
Anthologies: BlueGate Poets 2009 and 2010
Prize: Battered Moons

CHRISSY BANKS lives in Taunton, where she works as a counsellor and supervisor in private practice and is a member of Fire River Poets. She also runs a poetry reading group and occasional therapeutic writing days.
Book: *Days of Fire and Flood* (original plus)
Pamphlet: *Watching the Home Movies* (Odyssey Poets)
Anthologies include: *The Captain's Tower: Seventy Poets Celebrate Bob Dylan at Seventy* (Seren), *Only Connect* (Cinnamon), *Family Pictures* (Capital BookFest), *Eating Your Cake... and Having It* (Fatchance Press), *Poems Deep & Dangerous* (Cambridge University Press)
Magazines include: *The Rialto, Smiths Knoll, The Interpreter's House, South, Envoi, Obsessed with Pipework*
Prize: Grey Hen

HEIDI BECK lives in a village near Bath with her two children. She began writing poetry recently, after completing an MA in Creative Writing at Bath Spa University (concentrating on prose fiction). She is a member of the Knucklebone

Poets, a workshop group based in Bath. Born and raised in America, she also holds an MA in English Literature from the University of Chicago. She currently works as a tour guide in Bath.
Shortlist: Wells Festival of Literature

PAMELI BENHAM was born in London within the sound of Bow Bells and spent much of her adult life teaching toddlers, paratroopers, adolescents, prisoners and people with mental health problems, relieved by spells as a goose girl and growing citrus fruit in the Middle East. She now lives in Bristol where she writes, acts and directs. She has run a theatre company, taught writing and acting workshops, received a prize from UA Fanthorpe and had work performed by Show of Strength and displayed at St George's Bristol. Her collection of poems *Plentiful as Blackberries* was published by Poetry Can in 2012.

ZANNA BESWICK lives between Bath and Wells. She is a university lecturer and director in Drama and Theatre. For British television she has commissioned and/or produced more than 300 hours of broadcast drama and has trained a stable of writers and editors.
Anthologies: *In the Gold of Flesh* (The Women's Press), *The Ring of Words* (Telegraph Books), *Earth Ascending* (Stride), *3 x 4* (Raunchland Press),
Medley (Camden)
Magazines: *The Independent, Resurgence, Writing Women, Chrysalis, More to Life, Poetry Now, Camden Voices, Caduceus*
Prize: The Niai Foundation
Shortlists: Arvon International, Expressions of Encephalitis

AMA BOLTON is a founder-member of the Fountain Poets in Wells. In 2007 she edited and published their anthology *Poems from the Fountain*. Her hand-made books have been exhibited widely. In her spare time she cultivates her allotment or rides pillion on a powerful motorcycle. She is drawn to remote places, and visits the Northern Isles as often as she can.
Anthologies: *Up to Our Necks in It, The West Country, a Cultural History*, Bridport Prize anthology, Ver Poets anthology, *Hand Luggage Only*, Barnet Competition anthologies, British Haiku Society anthologies
Magazines: *Blithe Spirit, Snapshots, Echoes*
Prizes: Bridport, The Plough, Buxton Festival, Charnwood Mini-verse, Barnet Arts Council, Contemporary Poetry Haiku, Museum of Haiku Literature Award

JANICE BOOTH is a member of Swindon's BlueGate Poets She is twice winner of the Battered Moons competition and has had poems published in a number of local anthologies.Taking a determined view that 'if you don't try, you won't know', coupled with the feeling that time is always running out, she is consoled by the idea that the act of writing has the capacity to still or stall time. It can open up a sense of the eternal: a writer may focus on the everyday and, at the same time, escape from or dive deeper into it.

STEPHANIE BOXALL lives between Bath and Bristol. She has worked on national magazines and newspapers for more than 20 years and has an MA in Creative Writing from Bath Spa University where she concentrated on fiction writing. Three years ago she began writing poetry and joined a workshop in Oxford. Then she moved to Somerset and discovered the Bath Poetry Cafe. She has read her poems at the Bath Literature Festival, the Oxford Literary Festival and Oxford's Albion Beatnik Bookstore.

SUE BOYLE lives in Bath where she organises the Bath Poetry Cafe and the associated Festival events and Writing Days. She was a prizewinner in The Poetry Business Pamphlet Competition in 2009. For 20 years, she dealt in fine art and antique prints, drawings and paintings, and was a specialist maker of hand-finished picture frames.
Book: *Too Late for the Love Hotel* (Smith/Doorstop)
Anthologies: *Forward Poems of the Decade*, *Forward Anthology*
Magazines: *Poetry Ireland Review*, *The Rialto*, *Acumen*, *Magma*, *Poetry Salzburg*, *The Interpreter's House*
Prizes: *Wells Festival of Literature*, *Torbay Poetry Festival*

ELINOR BROOKS, originally from Edinburgh, is a founder member of Swindon's BlueGate Poets, and a sometime member of JETset – a trio of female poets who give readings. She works part-time as a lecturer in English and Creative Writing in a college of Further Education, where she also supports students with learning difficulties and disabilities.
Anthology: *Commonhead*
Magazines: *Pulsar*, *Domestic Cherry*, *the IMPpress*
Prize: Battered Moons
Shortlist: Borders Writers' Forum

SARA BUTLER lives in Somerset in the East Mendips. She taught English to overseas students for many years both in Norfolk and later at the University of Bath. While living in Norfolk she had an organic smallholding. She has been involved with the Bath Poetry Cafe for several years.

STEWART CARSWELL lives in Bristol where he is currently studying for a PhD in Physics. His poems are influenced by music, landscapes, and the manner of scientific exploration.
Magazine: *Obsessed with Pipework*

SUE CHADD lives in Malmesbury where she works part-time in the library. She organises poetry events locally and co-ordinates a convivial peer review group in a pub. A member of Swindon's BlueGate Poets, she has read her work on local radio, in libraries, at literature festivals, poetry cafés and charity events.
Books: *Vanishing Point* (National Poetry Foundation), *Releasing the Rook* (Applefire Press)

Anthologies include: *Common Source* (Anglo Welsh Poetry Society), *The Ticking Crocodile*, *Night Balancing, Cool and Quirky* (all Blinking Eye Publishing), Ver Poets anthology, *BlueGate Poetry Society*, *The Sunday Anthology*
Magazines: *Acumen, Borderlines, Graffiti, Iota, Pulsar, Second Light Newsletter, The Interpreter's House, The Journal* (once of Contemporary Anglo-Scandinavian Poetry), *Domestic Cherry, the IMPpress*
Prizes: Rosemary Arthur, Faringdon Poetry, Mere Literary Festival

ROSALIE CHALLIS studied languages in England, the US, Germany, Italy and France, where she lived during the Seventies, working as a secretary, teacher and book consultant. Later, in England, she worked on *The Good Book Guide*, becoming a director and Associate Editor. She joined the Bath Poetry Cafe workshop in 2009. She has taken part in readings at literature festivals in Bath and Wells, and in Faces, a video/audio show combining portraits and poetry. Learning the language of poetry has given her four challenging, exhilarating years.
Magazine: *Domestic Cherry*
Shortlist: Wells Festival of Literature

RACHAEL CLYNE lives in Glastonbury where she performs in a trio: Strange Sisters. She attends Wells Poetry Group and Bath Poetry Cafe. Rachael is a psychotherapist and has published self-help books. She is also an artist. As a professional actress, she performed with Erato and Angels of Fire poets.
Books: *She Who Walks with Stones and Sings* (PSAvalon), *Breaking the Spell –*
Keys to Recovering Self-esteem (PSAvalon)
Magazines: *Tears in the Fence, the IMPpress*
Prize: Sherborne Literary Festival
Shortlist: The Plough

DAVID COHEN has lived in Bath for more than 20 years. Originally a Londoner, he has worked as a theatre lighting designer, English teacher and ice-cream vendor. David has been writing poetry since his schooldays, but has recently been able to devote more time to his craft to reflect the wide range of his interests. He began writing with the Bath Poetry Cafe in 2012.

CLAIRE COLEMAN now lives in Somerset. For more than 20 years she has worked as a clown, Fool, juggler, created improvised physical theatre, toured with a circus, and taken her solo street shows to festivals in Australia and New Zealand. Currently she works part-time as a youth worker, a community tutor and also as a teacher of adults with disabilities. She was shortlisted for the Bradford-on-Avon poetry competition, and has taken part in readings at Bath Literature Festival and Wells Festival of Literature.

CLARE DIPROSE lives in north-east Somerset. Her poem Mammoth's Teeth won the Poetry Can competition in 1997. In 2009 she was a runner-up for the Bridport Poetry Prize and in 2011 came third in The Plough Prize. She is distracted by birds and islands, but group poetry sessions in Wells give her deadlines and encouragement. She is also a textile artist and a maker of books, some of which contain her poems.

Book: *Thinking of You* (Barley Books)
Anthologies: *A part or apart?*, *Poems from the Fountain*, The Bridport Prize anthology
Magazine: *Island*
Shortlists: The Bridport, The Plough

CLAIRE DYER wanted to be a BBC newsreader when she grew up. This clearly did not come to pass. Instead, she works part-time for an HR research forum in London, has been Clerk of The Worshipful Company of Management Consultants and is mother to two student sons. Her debut novel will be published by Quercus in October 2013.

Book: *Eleven Rooms* (Two Rivers Press)
Anthology: *Soul Feathers* (Indigo Dreams)
Magazines: *Other Poetry*, *Orbis*, *The Lampeter Review*, *Envoi*, *Domestic Cherry*
Prizes: Ware Poetry, York Open Poetry, Cinnamon Press Poetry

RAY FUSSELL lives in North Wraxall and is an original member of the Knucklebone Poets. He is a retired director of Plus One, a graphic design company based in Wotton-under-Edge. He currently guides visitors at Lacock Abbey and the American Museum in Bath.

BARRY GRANGER lives in Yate, where he is a service manager for a national CCTV company. A fully qualified FA coach, he fills his social time coaching at West Bromwich Albion's Gloucester Development Centre, playing saxophone and walking with his wife Denise. His son is a graphic designer in Greenwich and his daughter teaches Sports Science in Swindon. Barry joined the Bath Poetry Cafe in 2012, and these poems represent his first published work.

LOUISE GREEN lives in the West Country where she has facilitated creative writing courses for more than 20 years, working in both educational and healthcare settings. She has a particular interest in writing for wellbeing and is editor of *Lapidus Journal*. Her fiction has been broadcast on BBC Radio 4 and she has written for *The Guardian* and online journals. She now divides her time between her home in the Mendips and a small farmhouse in France, both places bringing inspiration to her writing.

Shortlist: Torbay Poetry Festival

DEBORAH HARVEY lives in Bristol. She is a trustee of Poetry Can and enjoys hill-walking with her border collie Ted.

Poetry Collection: *Communion* (Indigo Dreams)
Novel: *Dart* (Tamar Books)
Anthologies: *The World Is Made of Glass* and *Losing the Edge* (Ragged Raven), *Storm at Galesburg* (Cinnamon Press), *Dancing with Dulsie* (Leaf Books), *A Most Haunted Castle* (Longmarsh Press), Barnet Open Poetry Competition anthology, *The Genesis of Falcon and Other Winners* (Sentinel), Welsh Poetry Competition anthology

Magazines: *Mslexia, Writers' Forum, Salopeot, Sarasvati*
Prizes: Wells Festival of Literature, Pre-Raphaelite Society, Dor Kemmyn, Yeovil Literary Prize, Essex Poetry Festival, Staffordshire Poetry Competition, *Mslexia*, Poetry on the Lake, Sentinel, Welsh Poetry Competition, Chipping Sodbury Festival, Barnet Open Poetry Competition, Rhyme and Reason, Poetry Space

CAROLINE HEATON lives in Bath, where she works as a literature and creative writing tutor. She has performed her work in a variety of venues in Bath and Bristol and enjoys collaborating with artists in other media, regularly exhibiting with the Bear Flat Artists.
Books: *Close Company: Stories of Mothers and Daughters* (Virago), *Caught in a Story: Contemporary Fairytales and Fables* (Vintage), both co-edited with
Christine Park, *Yi-min and the Elephants* (Frances Lincoln Press)
Anthology: *Sparks: New Writing from Bath Spa University (Sulis Press)*
Magazines: *The Coffee House, Poetry in the Waiting Room, Domestic Cherry*

ROSIE JACKSON lives in rural Somerset where she writes and runs writing workshops. She left a successful academic career to follow the road less travelled, spent time in the USA and India, and believes passionately in the necessity of the creative arts for emotional and spiritual health. Her short stories have won awards and her poetry has been set for GCSE and made into a large sculpture in the grounds of a Dorchester hospital. She is now one of the Knucklebone Poets in Bath.
Books: *Fantasy: The Literature of Subversion, Frieda Lawrence, The Eye of the Buddha, Mothers Who Leave*
Magazines: *Acumen, Ambit, Poetry Salzburg, Tears in the Fence, The Interpreter's House, Domestic Cherry*
Prizes: Ambit, Writers Inc.

BERYL KELLOW lives in Berkshire and worked as a speech and language therapist for 40 years. She belongs to two writing groups and writes poetry and fiction; she enjoys life-writing. She was a runner-up in the Mere Literary Festival poetry section 2011 and gained honours in the Guernsey Eisteddfod poetry section 2011. Her work has appeared in the Whitehorse Writers' with Pennybank Writers' anthology 2011 the magazine: *Island Ink* and the BlueGate Poets' anthology 2012.

NIKKI KENNA lives in Wiltshire with her partner and son. A regular participant in the Bath Poetry Cafe, she also reads her poems in Swindon, Bradford-on-Avon and Frome, and is a founder member of Knucklebone Poets. In 2012, she helped co-ordinate the Bath Poetry Cafe's contribution to Voices in the City. Her first published poem appeared in *Domestic Cherry* in 2011. For 20 years, she worked in primary education and has edited poetry anthologies for children's publisher Barefoot Books. She likes drawing in Bath, watching peregrines in St Ives and paddling on Porthmeor beach.

MORAG KIZIEWICZ was born in Scotland and has lived in Somerset for most of the past 40 years. Her writing is inspired by a sense of 'ourselves in place'. Morag worked in Higher Education for more than 20 years, teaching spatial design at

Bournemouth Arts University College, then as Learning Support Manager at the University of Bath until she retired in 2009.

Books: *Dyslexia and Creativity* (Wiley), *Cascade: Creativity across Science, Art, Dyslexia and Education* (University of Bath), *Dyslexia and Stress* (Wiley),
Dyslexia and Visual Spatial Ability (Central St Martins)
Anthologies: *Dorset Waters*, *Dorset Contours* (East Street Poets)
Magazine: *Tears in the Fence*

EWAN MACPHERSON is a retired Anglican Priest living in Wells. He attends the Wells Poetry Group and the Bath Poetry Cafe. He served as a parish priest on Mendip for 20 years; before that, while living overseas, he earned a BA Hons in English Literature and an MDiv at the University of Toronto, and later served parishes in the Diocese.

Books: *Songs Before the Dawn*, *The Bridge of Moonlight* (The Halsgrove Press)
Prizes: University of Toronto Norma Epstein Prize for Poetry, US Fellowship
of Christian Poets Poet of the Year

LINDA PERRY lives in Nunney, Somerset, with her family and a three-acre garden. She has been involved in short story and poetry workshops, which have led to public readings at the Merlin Theatre and poetry cafés in Frome and Bath. After teaching English as a foreign language abroad she returned to the UK, and for the past 25 years has worked in catering and wholefoods, while bringing up a family and playing with words.

LESLEY SAUNDERS lives in Slough and Malmesbury. She has published several books and pamphlets of poetry and performed her work at festivals and on the radio. She has worked on collaborative projects with artists, sculptors, photographers and dancers, and her poems have been set to music by different musicians. She has held several residencies including one, in 2013, at the Museum of the History of Science, Oxford. She also works as an independent researcher in education and is a visiting professor at the Institute of Education, London.

Books: *Cloud Camera* (Two Rivers Press), *No Doves* (Mulfran Press), *Her Leafy Eye* (Two Rivers Press), *Christina the Astonishing* with Jane Draycott (Two Rivers Press)
Anthologies include: *In the Gold of Flesh*, *The West in Her Eye*, *Divers*, *A Mutual Friend: Poems for Charles Dickens* and the following prize anthologies: Arvon, Bridport, Forward and Hippocrates
Magazines include: *London Review of Books*, *Magma*, *Mslexia*, *Poetry Salzburg*, *Staple*, *Domestic Cherry*, *The Rialto*
Prizes include: Buxton Festival Poetry Competition, Manchester Poetry Prize,
Bath Roman Baths Competition, Staffordshire Poetry Competition special prize

LINDA SAUNDERS is a member of the International Association of Art Critics. An early spur to poetry was a wish for a more poetic language in which to speak about art. She reads regularly at the Bath Poetry Cafe and further afield. She divides her time between Bath and Ravenstonedale, Cumbria, and family commitments. She has eight grandchildren.

Books: *She River* (Vane Women Press), *Ways of Returning*, *The Watchers* (both Arrowhead)

Anthologies: *New Women Poets* (Bloodaxe), *The Green Book Anthology*
Magazines include: *Poetry Ireland Review, Poetry Review, The Warwick Review, Poetry Wales, The Rialto, Scintilla, Stand, Acumen, Agenda, The Interpreter's House, New Welsh Review, The Oxford Magazine, Smiths Knoll, Tears in the Fence,*
Other Poetry, Envoi
Prizes: Wells Festival of Literature, Salisbury House, Making Waves (for a poem on water)
Shortlists: Jerwood Aldeburgh First Collection Prize, BP Arts Journalist of the Year

LEANDA SENIOR lives in Weston-super-Mare, where she reads, writes and tries to write better. She has read her work and compèred events for the Bath Poetry Cafe in both Bath and Wells. She has worked as an academic administrator and lived in Japan.
Prize: Wells Festival of Literature

JILL SHARP is a former secretary of Swindon's BlueGate Poets. She works as an associate lecturer with the Open University and runs a local life-writing group. An anthology of work by group members was launched at the 2012 Swindon Festival of Literature.
Book: *Written in Stone* (English Heritage)
Anthologies: *Images of Women* (Arrowhead), *Pique* (Templar), *The World Is Made of Glass* (Ragged Raven), *Domestic Cherry*
Magazines: *Obsessed with Pipework, Fourteen, Mslexia, Poems in the Waiting Room, South, Ink Sweat & Tears, the IMPpress*
Prizes: Manchester Cathedral Poetry Prize, KUP War Writing Prize, Battered Moons
Shortlists: Virginia Warbey, Grace Dieu

SUSAN JANE SIMS lives in South Gloucestershire. She is the founder of Poetry Space Ltd, an independent publishing company specialising in printed and online poetry publications. She is also the administrator for Lapidus, the UK organisation for reading and writing for wellbeing, and a writer in schools for The Threshold Prize. Susan is currently developing an interest in performing her poetry and in 2013 took part in Bath Poetry Cafe's Voices in the City day.
Book: *Irene's Daughter* (Poetry Space Ltd)
Magazines: *Obsessed with Pipework, Reach, Sarasvati*
Anthologies: *Ice Blue Mornings, Crab Lines on the Pier, Visible Breath,*
Soul Feathers, Landscapes on the Edge, Heart Shoots
Prize: Bardic Writers' Circle
Shortlist: Poetry Pulse

SUSAN UTTING lives in Berkshire. She taught poetry and creative writing at Reading University and Randolph Macon College for 17 years. She now works freelance, tutoring creative writing undergraduates at Oxford University. She has appeared at major arts venues and poetry festivals including Aldeburgh, Ledbury, StAnza and Cheltenham.
Books: *Something Small Is Missing* (Smith/Doorstop), *Striptease* (Smith/Doorstop),
Houses Without Walls (Two Rivers Press), *Fair's Fair* (Two Rivers Press)

Anthologies include: *A Mutual Friend: Poems for Charles Dickens, The Captain's Tower: Seventy Poets Celebrate Bob Dylan at Seventy, Lyrical Beats, Images of Women, Domestic Cherry*, the Forward and Arvon Prize anthologies
Magazines include: *TLS, The Times, The Telegraph, The North, New Welsh Review, Mslexia*
Prizes include: Peterloo, Berkshire Poetry Prize, *The Times* Best Love Poems, Cardiff International
Shortlists include: Arvon, Bridport, National (longlist)

CATHY WILSON lives in Bristol, where she works, writes, and teaches poetry part-time. She is a regular reader at Bristol's Poetry Can Opener sessions and Bath Poetry Cafe, and has appeared at various arts venues and literature festivals, including Bath and Wells.
Anthologies: *Bristol Folk House Anthology* (City Chameleon), *Unsaid Words* (Trigger Editions)

SHIRLEY WRIGHT lives in Bristol. After a long and happy career as a French teacher, she now writes full-time. Her first novel came out in August 2012. She has a number of short stories in print, and her poetry collection *The Last Green Field* will be published in 2013 by Indigo Dreams.
Book: *Time out of Mind* (ThornBerry Publishing)
Anthologies: *The Impress Prize for New Writers*, The Ver Poets anthology, *Earthwords* (Friends of the Earth)
Magazines include: *Roundyhouse, The Interpreter's House, Poetry Monthly International, The French Literary Review, Equinox, Other Poetry*
Prizes: Wells Festival of Literature, *The Sunday Telegraph*/Rose Theatre Poetry for Performance Competition, *The Times* Halloween Ghost Story Competition

JEREMY YOUNG lives in Somerset, where he is in private practice as a systemic psychotherapist working with individuals, couples and families. He has worked as a parish priest in the Church of England and in theological education in Dublin. He has published two books on psychology and religion, *The Cost of Certainty* and *The Violence of God and the War on Terror* (Darton, Longman & Todd).
Anthologies: *New Christian Poetry* (Collins Flame), *Extended Wings 3, 4, & 5* (Rathmines Writers/Swan Press), *Quintet* (Swan Press), *The Ingredients of Poetry* (Riposte Books), *Ireland's Love Poems* (Kyle Cathie)
Magazines: *Acumen, The Interpreter's House, Other Poetry, Orbis, Poetry Ireland Review*
Prizes: Surrey Poetry Centre, Riposte

The cover artist
Malcolm Ashman

Bath Poetry Cafe is grateful to Malcolm Ashman for permission to use *Chalk Down, Dorset* on the cover of *The Listening Walk*.

Malcolm Ashman was born in Bath in 1957 and studied at Somerset College of Art. He is a member of the Royal Society of British Artists (RBA), the Royal Institute of Oil Painters (ROI) and the Bath Society of Artists. His numerous exhibitions include solo shows at the Brian Sinfield Gallery in the Cotswolds, Beaux Arts in Bath and Denise Yapp Contemporary Art in Monmouthshire. His awards include the Andrew Brownsword Prize at the Victoria Art Gallery, Bath, the Alan Gourley Memorial Award, the Bridge Macfarland Prize, the Cornelissen Prize, the Davison Award and *The Artist* Magazine Award at the Mall Galleries, London.

Essentially a landscape painter in the romantic tradition, Ashman is strongly influenced by the rolling countryside of his native West Country. Colour, shape and imagination all come into play here, which gives his work a unique quality. Brian Sinfield, Brian Sinfield Gallery, Oxfordshire

I enjoy being in the landscape, but it's the recollection of that experience which makes me a painter. Brief line drawings from observation are a starting point, but the paintings are formed in the studio from memory and imagination. Malcolm Ashman

Index

Made in the USA
Charleston, SC
11 May 2013